Sussex Haunted Heritage

Historic Properties Open to the Public

Debra Munn

S.B. Publications

For my dad, John Dee Munn,
who died while I was writing this book,
but whose spirit continues to love and watch over me.

First published in 2006 by S. B. Publications
Tel: 01323 893498
Email: sbpublications@tiscali.co.uk

ISBN 185770 318 9

Designed and Typeset by EH Graphics (01273) 515527
Printed by Ethos Productions Ltd.

Contents

Acknowledgements

First I want to acknowledge the continuing presence in my life of my own dear family and friends who have recently passed away: my dad, John Munn; my aunts Virgie Irving, Frances Cyrus and Elizabeth Carter; my uncle, Rex Carter; my cousin Butch Pryor; and friends Gordon Thake, Dodi Vaughn, Harry Britt and Marilyn Osborne. All but Butch lived a long life, but we weren't ready to let any of them go. I'd like to send up my love and appreciation to all of them for their love, friendship, encouragement to keep writing, and just for being themselves! I also want to express my gratitude and appreciation to the late Steve Benz, founder of S. B. Publications, for his enthusiasm for this book and for giving me the initial go-ahead, and to his sister, Lindsay Woods, for her patience, understanding and guidance as I completed the project. My thanks also go to photo editor Liz Howe.

Thanks are also due to everyone who responded to my requests for information about haunted, historic places in Sussex. In addition to everyone mentioned in the chapters, I would like to thank the following, without whom I could never have completed this book: Caroline Adams, West Sussex Records Office; Kim Rose-Alison; Julia Appleby, Bognor Open Mind; Rosemary Baird, Goodwood House; Caroline Barnett, SE England Tour Guide; John Bleach, Lewes Castle; Joyce Brouitt, The National Trust; Hilary Cassidy, Spectrum in Worthing; Paul Coomber, Bayham Abbey; Colin Dartnell, *The Kingston News*; Geoff Dent; Allan Downend; Josephine DuBern; Derek Ellwood; Esme Evans, Sussex Archaeological Society Library; Ray Fitzgerald; Ken Francis; Val Fryer, Sussex Archaeological Society; Rebecca Graham, Nymans Garden; Carol Griffiths, Blue Badge Guide; Susan Hamblin, *South Today;* Alison Hardy, Groombridge Place Gardens; Sabrina Holland; Ann Humphries; Ron Iden, West Sussex Records Office; Liz Jordan, Pevensey Castle; Jeremy Knight, Horsham Museum; Chris Layen; Michael Leppard, East Grinstead Town Museum; Jane Lunnon; Barbara Maidment, Groombridge Place Gardens; Christine Maynard, Fernhurst Archive; Derek Mortimer, The Dickens Fellowship; Chris Munns, Sussex Archaeological Society; Jon S. Page, Augustus Hare Society; Sarah Philp; Helen Poole, Sussex Archaeological Society; Brian Pugh, Conan Doyle Establishment, Crowborough; Jenny Quest; Sara Rodger; Anita Rogers, Nymans Garden; Tallulah Sandilands, Pevensey Court House Museum & Jail; Victoria Seymour; Ann Spike, Lewes District Council; Ian Topham, www.mysteriousbritain.co.uk; Robert Wainwright; Tony Wales; Tony Willliams, The Dickens Fellowship; Amanda Wilson.

Thanks also to my mother, Bonnie Munn, and to my husband, Mick Henry, just for being there and for being so loving and supportive.

Introduction

Many books about Sussex ghosts have been written over the years, but as far as I know, this is the first to focus solely upon haunted historic properties that the public may visit. And as there are probably hundreds of churches, pubs, and other kinds of buildings accessible to the public that qualify in some way as both 'haunted' and 'historic', I have further limited the scope of this book to properties that have served at one time or other as residences, or at least part-time habitations - for living people as well as ghosts! Another criterion is that these places, or at least parts of them, had to be attractions or museums opened as such, and not used solely for other purposes - as hotels, restaurants, or shops, for example. I made exceptions to this rule whenever I found supernatural phenomena from the main property I was researching that seemed to 'spill over' onto secondary sites adjacent to or in some way connected to the primary one. If these occurrences seemed linked in some way to the main property, I included them, too.

To start my research, I contacted owners, caretakers or staff of all the Sussex properties fitting my criteria (at least those that still have anyone left to contact!) and then interviewed as many people as I could find who had had supernatural experiences themselves at the sites, or who were at least familiar with the stories there. Wherever possible, I have used real names, and where not permitted to do so, I have identified people only in general terms, or occasionally by a first name only. I would like to thank all those who helped me with my research at these historic properties, as I could never have completed this book without them.

I am also much indebted to the writers who have gone before me in chronicling Sussex ghost tales. I combed through stacks of books, magazines, newspapers, brochures, and other printed sources in search of relevant material, and I also spent a great deal of time surfing the internet for websites devoted both to historic buildings and to tales of the paranormal in the county. As my goal was to provide as full a rendering as possible of the unexplained phenomena from the various properties, I have tried not only to update but also to present a composite of accounts from other authors. Where there is general agreement among them regarding the details of occurrences at a particular place, I have not cited individual sources. But I have done so whenever a writer is the only one to tell a tale or to provide information that doesn't appear elsewhere. I have also included links to websites showing images of purported phenomena at certain sites. All URLs were accurate at the time of writing, but are subject to change. I would encourage interested readers to seek out for themselves the previously published books about Sussex ghosts, as all of them lend something unique to the subject.

It would probably be helpful here for me to explain my own favourite theories about ghosts. The most common belief, of course, is that they are conscious spirits of the dead who, for reasons of their own, return to places they knew as living beings. Certainly many accounts of the supernatural seem to involve entities of this type, but another very plausible theory is that what we call 'ghosts' may instead be impressions that have somehow been recorded on the physical environment during times of crisis or heightened emotions, good or bad. If that is true, these hauntings are like tape-recorded material that is available for playback under the appropriate (although still not understood) conditions. This theory would account not only for the sighting of some apparitions that appear again and again in the same place, but also for ghostly noises or even phantom odours. In this collection of stories, readers must judge for themselves about the nature of the phenomena involved, but to me, it appears that both theories make sense, and that both kinds of 'ghosts' are indeed present in the haunted, historic buildings of Sussex.

At the time of writing, all these properties were regularly open to the public or at least expected to be at the time of the book's publication; but as circumstances might change, those wishing to visit should always check first on opening times. Some of the sites are free to visit, while others charge an entrance fee. Some allow public access both inside and out, while others allow only a stroll around the grounds. Some of them, such as Bramber and Knepp Castles, are now merely ruins; and in the case of Cowdray House and Park Ruins, visitors are usually not permitted to tour the site itself, but are allowed close enough access to get a good look. And one of these places - Verdley Castle - is practically a ghost itself nowadays, so much so that would-be visitors will have a real challenge even to find where it once stood!

While my goal has been to find and write about all the haunted, historic properties open to the public in Sussex, I'm sure that I might have missed one or two. I'm equally sure that I probably failed to track down all the stories set in this place or that - I was certainly surprised to find no stories from Petworth, Parham House or Standen, for example. And since new psychic occurrences might be taking place even as I write these words, no book of ghost stories, including this one, can ever be complete. Neither can I guarantee the accuracy of any of these supposedly 'true' tales, but I have tried to present them as fully, clearly, and interestingly as possible, leaving the matter of belief up to you, the reader. So I hope that this book will inform, delight, and entertain, and also that it will inspire within you a new appreciation for the supernatural in Sussex.

Alfriston Clergy House
ALFRISTON, EAST SUSSEX

ince so many National Trust properties are haunted, it's only appropriate that the very first building acquired by the organisation should have a ghost - or ghosts, as the case may be. For if all the sightings and strange occurrences at this fourteenth-century former priest's house are caused by a lone phantom, he (and everyone agrees, at least, that it is a 'he') is a very busy one indeed, appearing in costumes from different periods of history and engaging in a number of peculiar pastimes!

But no one could blame a spirit (or spirits) for lingering at this lovely timber-framed house, built around 1350 and purchased by the National Trust for only £10 in 1896. Alfriston itself, although plagued in recent years by heavy tourist traffic, is the kind of quintessential English village that could have been lifted out of a fairy tale. The thatched Clergy House, nestling up to the Cuckmere River and adjacent to the Parish Church of St Andrew, helps make the illusion complete.

Today it is difficult to imagine these two buildings in any other setting. But local lore says that the church was originally intended to lie west of the village street. When construction began, however, a mysterious, unseen force toiled night after night to hurl the newly laid stones onto the green known as the Tye. All attempts to erect the church in the first location proved futile. Then someone noticed four oxen lying rump to rump on the Tye, their bodies forming a cross. The frustrated workmen perceived this as a sign from Providence that a cruciform church was to be built on that very spot. A. Cecil Piper, recounting this legend in his pamphlet, *The Parish Church of St. Andrew, Alfriston,* admits that it is a lovely story, but questions it since it is also told about Durham Cathedral and other houses of worship. A variation on the theme appears in Tony Wales's *Sussex Ghosts & Legends.* Wales suggests that the being who removed the builders' stones was not God, but the devil (Newbury, Berkshire: Countryside Books, 1992, 7).

However one regards the tale, it does show that the supernatural has long been associated with this most beautiful corner of Alfriston. And judging from reports over the years, that association has continued up to recent times, especially with the Clergy House, although current staff members have refused to say whether they have experienced anything of a paranormal nature there. In 1980, Andrew Green wrote that the building was believed to be haunted by a former inhabitant, who appeared 'in the shape of an old man in a tattered grey suit' *(Ghosts of Today,* London: Kaye & Ward, 35). Green went on to say that in 1974 a custodian told him that a previous official had seen the apparition 'many years earlier', before renovation work was carried out, but Green wondered whether the spectre had in fact been seen since then, only to be mistaken for a living individual.

Ghosts who look solid and 'real' and who dress and act like people of the present decade might indeed pass as live humans, but former staff members of the Clergy House had no doubts as to the otherworldly status of the being *they* encountered during their time there in the late 1990s. Former custodian Nick Jarvis and volunteer Shelley Bernard recalled that they often smelled the strong odour of a cigar wafting just outside the house, usually early in the morning. Yet smoking of all kinds is prohibited on National Trust property, and no 'culprit' was ever found. Shelley Bernard also reported feeling the invisible presence of someone in the Hall, an experience that caused shivers to race down her spine.

'Some say it could be a nobleman from a past century who used to be in the house,' she explained. 'I don't know who it is, but it's definitely a man. And people have said that if it's the same one who smokes the cigars, then he has to be at least wealthy enough to afford such things.'

Nick Jarvis and fellow worker Joan Dyer also recalled hearing footsteps overhead when the house was closed and they were sure no one was upstairs. But the most spectacular accounts come from Jack Baylis, who is retired now but who was in charge of visitor reception at the Clergy House for eight years. On a dark, misty afternoon in the early 1990s, Jack had just returned to the main house from the shop when he was stunned by the apparition of a man only five yards away in the Hall.

'I clearly saw this figure,' Jack insisted. 'He was dressed as a nineteenth-century customs and excise man - the kind who used to chase smugglers - with a sword, knee-length boots, and black cloak. He looked like a real, flesh-and-blood human, and I stood absolutely still for two or three minutes, staring at him and wondering if I was imagining things. I thought, that's definitely someone from another century. His face didn't change, and he didn't appear to notice me. He was still, like a cardboard cutout, but then he moved across the Hall and vanished through the wooden pillar that supports the roof.'

On another dark, misty day around the same time, Jack watched what appeared to be a vessel from a bygone age making its way up the Cuckmere just behind the house. 'These things always seem to happen when the light's fading,' he admitted, 'but I clearly heard a dog barking and the sound of people's voices, and I looked out to see what appeared to be one of those smuggling barges that used to bring contraband from France. They unloaded them in Alfriston and then hid the goods in big cellars under the houses. I can't tell if what I saw was a real barge or not, but it was certainly an unusual sight for the 1990s, and very unusual at any time of the day for such a large boat to be coming up the river. It was high tide and very misty, with only a few people about, and it was a very strange sensation hearing this dog barking and people's voices on the boat.'

Since some of the strange phenomena at the Alfriston Clergy House seem connected to smuggling, it's tempting to wonder whether phantom practitioners might not get up to their old tricks from time to time in the shop. In the spring of 1997, former shop manager Margaret Edwards experienced several odd occurrences.

'We sold National Trust picnic sets,' she said, 'and one day a bottle opener disappeared from one of them. I asked the staff if anyone had sold it, but everyone said no. So I decided it had been pinched and thought no more about it. But a few weeks later, the bottle opener reappeared in the picnic set - only this time the corkscrew was missing! I asked everyone in the shop if it had been sold, but again the answer was no.'

All-too-human thieves or pranksters could be at fault here, although that didn't seem likely to Margaret. And she was just as perplexed as to how a pile of napkins that had been stacked and wedged inside a partially opened dresser drawer somehow ended up on the floor, apparently without the aid of human hands. Books, likewise, unaccountably tumbled from their shelves, even after being secured by staff to prevent them from falling on customers' heads.

I witnessed the flying-book phenomenon myself in May 1997, before I even knew that the Clergy House was haunted. Coincidentally, I was waiting at the till to buy Andrew Green's *Haunted Sussex Today*, thinking about my own plans to write this book and wondering which chapter to research first. Just as I was about to hand over my money, a large book suddenly plummeted from the top of a cabinet next to me and onto the floor.

'It's the ghost again!' said the man at the till.

A ghost? Or just a perfect example of synchronicity? Whichever it was, I'm grateful - for surely there could have been no more delightful spot to begin my research than at the charming Alfriston Clergy House.

Anne of Cleves House
LEWES, EAST SUSSEX

nne of Cleves, the fourth wife of Henry VIII, may have been given this timber-framed Wealden hall-house as part of a divorce settlement in 1541, but she almost certainly never visited it during her lifetime, or, as far as anyone knows, after her death. For even though the Anne of Cleves House in Lewes has two ghost stories connected with it, neither, apparently, involves the lady for whom the house is named.

In fact, the events surrounding the first story occurred long before the sixteenth century when the house was built (although some parts of it may be older). On 29 December 1170, as all students of English history know, the Archbishop of Canterbury, Thomas Becket, was slain in Canterbury Cathedral by four assassins under the orders of Henry II. Following the horrific murder, the killers fled from Kent into Sussex, where on the second night they reached a college of Benedictine canons called Malling House in Southover, Lewes.

Upon entering the house, Becket's murderers discarded their bloody swords onto a large table that stood in the hall. They had supper and afterwards gathered around a blazing hearth to discuss the ramifications of what they had done. Their hushed tones were suddenly interrupted by a loud clatter as the table where they had laid the vile instruments reared back and hurled them onto the floor.

Attendants hearing the commotion rushed in with flaming torches and replaced the arms. But soon an even louder crash occurred as the massive table juddered convulsively and once again pitched the swords onto the floor. Servants and soldiers ran into the hall again, searching everywhere to discover the cause of the disturbance. Finally, one of the conscience-stricken knights spoke up. He was certain that the table, which had often been used by Becket himself, was refusing to support the sacrilegious weapons that had taken the archbishop's life.

As late as the fourteenth century, the table was said to have been visited by pilgrims to Malling House. At some time afterwards, it was taken to the Anne of Cleves House, where it remains a favourite with visitors such as Prince Edward, who, familiar with the story, came to see the legendary table in 2002.

But could this sturdy octagonal piece of furniture with its grey Sussex marble top really have played such an important role in history? Most visitors to the Anne of Cleves House would probably like to believe that it did, but Tony Wales in *A Treasury of Sussex Folklore* claims that unfortunately, 'the date given to the table by experts conflicts with the period of the legend' (Seaford, Sussex: S.B. Publications, 2000, 8).

Even so, the site of the old Malling House, where the legendary events supposedly occurred, has itself had repeated hauntings over the years, although none seems to have anything to do with the agitated table or with the assassins of Thomas Becket. The original Malling House was demolished during Henry VIII's Dissolution of the Monasteries, but the present building, not open to the public, was probably built around 1660, rebuilt in 1720, and is believed to stand on the same spot - and how ironic that the site that once housed the most famous fugitives in Sussex history should now be the headquarters for the county's police force!

An article by Phil Mills in *The Argus* on 16 August 2000 details the encounters of officers and other staff with a ghost called Annie, also referred to as the 'grey lady' or 'lady of the rose garden' (so nicknamed because she was often seen tending the flowers outside the building when she was alive). Annie is believed to have been a maid who became pregnant by the householder's son, and who 'accidentally' fell down a flight of stairs before she could give birth. A former police constable caught a glimpse of her walking past a door one night in 1981, and in another occurrence, a secretary claimed that her office went cold right before a very solid-seeming woman appeared, wearing a long, greyish white dress and frilly cap. Even more alarming, a cleaner was forced to yell for help on several occasions when the door to a cupboard mysteriously slammed shut, trapping her inside.

Back at the Anne of Cleves House, senior custodian Steve Watts claims to have sensed the presence of a much more accommodating spirit, especially in the upstairs bedroom.

'It's as if somebody is looking after the house,' he told me. 'I often feel somebody on my shoulder. It's certainly not scary in any way, and I think that someone clears up after me. I'm convinced that sometimes when I go up to the bedroom in the morning, it's in a tidier state than when I left it the night before. If there is a ghost up there, she's not the type who messes things up - she likes to dust and rearrange the chairs slightly to make the room look nicer.'

Any spirit who lavishes such care upon her surroundings probably loved them well in life, and this thought adds poignancy to the tragic story Steve told me next. 'There have been possibly a dozen different sightings of a person dressed in white, hanging from one of the timbers of the room,' he said. 'Most people believe that it's a small child, but there is historic evidence that the ghost is probably that of an elderly lady who hanged herself off the beams in 1834, when the house was bought by the local Verrall's Brewery just down the road. They had bought the building to house their workers, but as the elderly lady was a washerwoman and not employed by the brewery, she was going to be evicted from her home. She was obviously desolate, with nowhere else to go, so she hanged herself.

'As she was old and very poor, she was probably malnourished and quite small. I believe that's why people think that what they're seeing is a child. The sightings happen on a regular basis. Some visitors come downstairs looking very upset and leave the museum straight away. Many people get a cold feeling in the room.'

Various paranormal investigators have also sensed a presence in the bedroom, and some American visitors reported 'a distinct cold spot over by the headboard' (see their website at http://www.delcoghosts.com/Anne.html). A mysterious white orb shows at the top of a photo they took inside the room.

So although Anne of Cleves herself has yet to make a spectral appearance at her namesake house in Lewes, there are still enough supernatural elements there to satisfy even the most demanding spook hunter - or even the casual tourist just looking for a charming spot to spend a day out!

𝕬rundel 𝕮astle
ARUNDEL, WEST SUSSEX

Inside the back cover of John Martin Robinson's recent *Arundel Castle* guidebook is a statement by Winefride Freeman on the subject of ghosts. Born at the castle in 1914, this lady lived there for twenty-two years, but saw nary a spook nor spectre. Furthermore, she said, some of the tales told now were never mentioned in her youth.

Be that as it may, visitors on the lookout for the supernatural have no reason to shun the second largest castle in England, for ghostly tales - even some fairly recent ones - do abound there. In fact, it would be very strange if they did not, for Arundel Castle has stood for nearly a thousand years and has provided the setting for both turbulent and triumphant episodes in English history.

In fact, the oldest ghost at this castle is most likely that of its builder, Roger de Montgomery, who fought alongside his cousin William the Conqueror at the Battle of Hastings. For his services Roger was rewarded with the Earldoms of Shrewsbury and Arundel, along with the rape of Chichester, making him Lord of no fewer than eighty-four manors. The Earl founded the original Arundel Castle on Christmas Day 1067, and some say that his ghost still watches benignly over the magnificent keep.

Apart from a few occasions when the castle for political reasons reverted to the Crown, from the twelfth century to the present it has been occupied by members of the same family. Passed down by a succession of female heiresses, Arundel Castle has been in turn the home of the d'Albinis, the Fitzalans, and the Howards, and through the latter, the seat of the Dukes of Norfolk for over five hundred years.

During the Civil War, the castle was claimed by the Royalists, and from late December 1643 to early January 1644, it was besieged by the Parliamentarian general, Sir William Waller. Some say that Waller's cannons may still be heard booming from time to time, making the walls reverberate just as they did over three hundred and fifty years ago. Damaged during the siege, the castle was left unrestored until the nineteenth century, when it underwent two periods of reconstruction. The fairy-tale appearance of Arundel Castle today results largely from this latter rebuilding, which, however, apparently failed to remove the ghosts.

The best known of all Arundel Castle apparitions is the Blue Man who frequents the library, mostly at night. Usually described as a Cavalier or dandy wearing blue silk, he has also been said to wear velvet or corduroy. Most chroniclers say that his clothing dates from the time of Charles II, although others claim that the spectre must be from a period a few decades before that, as the first sighting, they explain, took place as early as the 1630s.

If the first sighting did happen that early, we are left wondering about the setting, for the library as it exists today was not completed until about 1800. (We might also question why or even how a ghost could appear in a room that didn't exist during his lifetime. If ghosts are free wandering spirits, able to go wherever they wish through time and space, this would not be a problem. If they are, however, merely some kind of recorded impressions on the environment, such a thing would be impossible.) But let's turn away from theory and get back to the legend, which says that the Blue Man is usually seen seated, poring intently over a book, or browsing eagerly through various volumes as if in search of some important bit of information.

For his *Haunted Sussex Today*, Andrew Green interviewed a custodian who was intrigued by his encounter with the Blue Man in the late 1990s. Not at all frightened, the custodian was actually disappointed when the scholarly spectre vanished after being observed for a good minute or so (Seaford, East Sussex: S.B. Publications, 1997, 9-10).

Another library ghost reported by Green is that of a small black dog, seen so far only by children. The dog is said to have belonged to St Philip Howard, Earl of Norfolk, who was sentenced to death for failing to renounce his Roman Catholic faith. The sentence was never carried out, but the saintly Earl was imprisoned in the Tower of London when a rumour circulated that he had led a public mass for the success of the Spanish Armada against his own country. He spent ten years in the Tower, accompanied by his faithful pet, until he died in 1595. Some claim that he died of dysentery, while others say that he was poisoned. Later he was beatified, and in 1970 was canonised as a saint by Pope Paul VI. It is unclear why (or how, as mentioned previously) his dog would haunt the library at Arundel Castle, but guides there have said that children often ask about the owner of the small animal they see running about.

Kitchen staff have occasionally reported run-ins with the phantom of a scullion who may still be heard, and more rarely seen, vigorously scrubbing pots and pans. Believed to have been a serving lad at the castle in the eighteenth century, the young man was routinely bullied by a cruel cook or head cellarer, who beat him to death one day as punishment for slovenly work. The story is that pots and pans are sometimes heard rattling around the kitchen at night, long after staff members have gone to bed. According to some versions of the tale, at one point in the twentieth century, kitchen staff even left out cleaning pans overnight, hoping that the ghost would put his frantic energy to good use!

An altogether quieter phantom was seen in 1958 in another part of the servants' quarters. A trainee footman was on his way to turn off the lights of the drawbridge around eleven o'clock one night. As he headed toward the main switch box located on the ground floor corridor, he became aware that someone was about fifteen feet ahead of him, moving in the same direction. Drawing nearer, he saw an apparition of a man whose head and shoulders were dressed in a light grey tunic with loose sleeves. The figure seemed to be in his mid-twenties, with long hair. The witness described the phantom's image as similar to an old photo, with a blurred outline. He was unable to see anything below waist level, as the light was low. As he kept walking, the phantom seemed to fade and then vanished completely, having appeared for only about thirty seconds. The witness claimed that before his encounter with the spectre, he'd never heard any of the castle ghost stories and wouldn't have been interested in them, anyway. But his experience so alarmed him that he ran back along the corridor, forgetting to switch off all the lights.

An even more alarming apparition, at least to members of the Howard family, is that of the white bird fluttering against the castle windows when one of their members is about to die. It's important to mention that many old, historic families have similar omens of death, and that throughout Sussex, a screech-owl is considered a traditional messenger of evil. According to some versions of the tradition, the ghostly harbinger at Arundel Castle is described as a small white bird, but others hold that the tragic messenger is really a white owl. The latter version ties in with the fact that before the restoration of the castle keep in the nineteenth century, the Dukes of Norfolk kept an aviary of owls there. Regardless of the species, the story is that a ghostly white bird made its appearance just before the death of the Duke of Norfolk in 1917.

Another white ghost, or more specifically, a white lady, is believed to haunt Hiorne's Tower, built on top of a ridge about a kilometre north-west of the castle. This legend tells us that the sorrowful young woman, dressed all in white, may be seen on still, moonlit nights. She stands at the top of this eighteenth-century tower, looking in vain for her beloved. A victim of a tragic love affair, the despairing woman is commonly believed to have plunged to her death from Hiorne's Tower, although some say that she hurled herself from one of the towers of the castle itself.

The tour of Arundel Castle and its grounds also includes the nearby Fitzalan Chapel and the adjoining St Nicholas parish church, originally divided as a result of a legal dispute. An iron grille today separates the two parts, but both have been the setting during recent decades for supernatural phenomena.

Most famous was an incident in 1940, in which an Arundel solicitor accidentally captured a ghost on film while photographing the altar of St Nicholas church. As he had been the only person in the building when he took the photo, the solicitor was shocked when the developed print showed what appeared to be the back of a somewhat transparent, robed priest standing or kneeling at the altar. The picture has been reproduced in a number of books and may be viewed on the web at http://www.geocities.com/petesghosts/ghostsonfilm2.html.

A spectral nun in grey was seen twice in the church during the same decade. The town crier was in the habit of visiting the church to wind the clock, and on one occasion he saw the ghost of the young nun seated in a chair. She remained there for a few minutes before both she and the chair vanished. Nine months later the town crier again had an encounter with the phantom sister, this time on the stairway landing of the bell tower. Behind this landing an oak door led on to a small platform that was possibly used as a lookout during the Civil War. Some have conjectured that the phantom was that of a young nun from a nearby convent who had either fallen or jumped from the platform.

After the doorway was blocked up, there were no more reports of a ghost in the bell tower, at least until December 1995 when a bell-ringer ascending the stairs became aware that he was not alone. Not only did he sense the presence of another person in front of him - he also clearly heard footsteps.

It is unclear whether the ghost that the bell-ringer encountered was that of the young nun, but a churchwarden may have seen her praying in a pew in the Fitzalan Chapel. He, too, claimed to see a phantom woman in grey. He then called out to his wife, and together they watched the praying woman until she gradually dissolved before their eyes.

Andrew Green in the aforementioned *Haunted Sussex Today* describes other eerie incidents in the chapel. In the late 1970s a churchwarden happened to glimpse a woman kneeling at the altar. She had white hair and was wearing a long blue gown. Assuming her to be a member of the Howard family, the churchwarden left the building quietly and told one of the gardeners outside what he had seen. The gardener explained that no one could possibly have been inside, as that part of the chapel was locked. The gardener then produced the key from his own pocket. The two men hurried back inside to make sure that the door was truly locked. It was, of course, and no one was inside the chapel.

Green goes on to tell about the experience of a woman visiting the Fitzalan Chapel in 1983. While looking at the marble effigies, she felt herself particularly drawn toward one of a woman wearing an Elizabethan dress. This effigy was on a tomb in one of the side aisles, and the woman said that she felt a strange and sudden rapport with it. Her husband, on the other hand, suddenly felt extremely cold and suffered such a strong feeling of antagonism that he was forced to leave. Three years later, Green says, two friends of the couple visited the chapel and admitted that they had also left in a hurry, feeling that area to be very uncomfortable and even aggressive.

Most visitors to Arundel Castle report no such uncomfortable feelings from the ghosts, however, or from anything else in the grounds. In fact, there is probably no more delightful place to go for a day's outing in all of Sussex, or all of England, for that matter. The country's second largest castle is second to none when it comes to beauty, charm, and an almost palpable sense of history.

Bateman's
BURWASH, EAST SUSSEX

Bateman's, a grey stone house built in 1634, was the beloved home of the writer Rudyard Kipling and his wife Caroline, who moved to this idyllic Sussex retreat in 1902. At the age of thirty-six, Kipling was the world's most famous author, and he was looking for a place to escape from the pressures of fame. He and Caroline were also still in mourning for their daughter, Josephine, who had died of pneumonia just three years before.

Both Kiplings fell in love with Bateman's the first time they saw it. Kipling describes their first impression of the house in his posthumously published autobiography, *Something of Myself*. In Chapter VII, 'The Very-Own House', he writes, 'We entered and felt her Spirit - her Feng Shui - to be good. We went through every room and found no shadow of ancient regrets, stifled miseries, nor any menace, though the "new" end of her was three hundred years old' (1937). Upon speaking to the owner, the Kiplings were disappointed to learn that Bateman's had just been let for a year. Twelve months later, however, when the house was advertised again, they wasted no time in buying it and making it their own.

One of the most evocative parts of the house is Kipling's study, where, inspired by the Sussex countryside, he wrote *Puck of Pook's Hill* and enjoyed many happy hours smoking and working until his death in 1936. The study has been left almost exactly as it was during his lifetime, as stipulated by Caroline when she left Bateman's to the National Trust upon her death just a few years after her husband's. Visitors to the room, as well as former guides at Bateman's, have often reported the strong feeling of a presence in the study, or the sensation that Kipling himself has just popped out for a few moments. Others have claimed to feel a strong sense of energy and vitality.

In 1975, when members of the Ghost Club paid a visit to Bateman's, one of them, John Harvey, had a most unsettling experience in the study. Harvey considered himself to be one of the more practical members of the group, and he rarely experienced anything of a supernatural nature. Yet as he looked into Kipling's workplace, he saw clearly the figure of the writer himself, appearing alive and solid, gazing thoughtfully out of the window. Although Harvey was astounded, he stood quietly watching the figure, and had just decided to speak to him when another member of the Ghost Club wandered into the room. Harvey was on the verge of pointing out the great man to his friend when the apparition suddenly vanished (see Peter Underwood, *This Haunted Isle: The Ghosts and Legends of Britain's Historic Buildings,* Javelin Books: Poole, New York, Sidney, 1986, 22-23, and Andrew Green, *Haunted Sussex Today,* Seaford, East Sussex: S.B. Publications, 1997, 26).

Andrew Green claims that other visitors, as well as some of the guides at Bateman's, also admitted seeing Kipling's ghost in the study, usually gazing out of the window as he was when John Harvey saw him. Peter Underwood writes of one witness who was strongly aware of the presence of someone with 'enormous enthusiasm and energy' in various rooms but especially in the study 'at dusk'.

Current staff members told me that they were unaware of any recent supernatural occurrences in the study or elsewhere. Nevertheless, they explained that because both the Kiplings had imprinted their personalities so firmly on their home, a feeling of their continued presence was therefore only to be expected. Perhaps, as Underwood reports, that explains why a Mrs Lees who lived at Bateman's in the 1940s told the administrator in 1982 that she had always felt especially uneasy in the Kiplings' bedroom.

The observation of eerie presences at Bateman's isn't limited to the house, however. The phantoms of both Rudyard and Caroline Kipling, but especially Carrie, have been seen among the flowers in the garden that they loved so well and worked so hard to improve. Both Green and Underwood report that a former custodian was told that one, or perhaps two people had seen the figure of Carrie Kipling in the garden. In Green's account, she was said to be tending the flowers. In Underwood's, she was observed walking at night in the garden, carrying a basket that she liked to sit on. But the custodian's wife had her doubts about the accuracy of the tale, as the witness was believed to be drunk at the time of the sighting!

Apparently no such excuse can account for the story of the ghastly ghost lurking not far from Bateman's in Gladwish (or Glydwish) Wood. Kipling wrote that for him, the wood was full of 'a sense of ancient ferocity and evil', and admitted to R. Thurston Hopkins, who wrote a biography of Kipling, that sometimes, while taking an evening walk through it, he 'felt a secretive and menacing feeling all around me, holding me expectant and always on guard. In that evil wood everything is evil'.

Not that the woods were lonely, Kipling insisted, but that 'there's too much life there: a kind of ill-natured and venomous life. There is a spirit of some kind there for one evening something suddenly gripped me and despite my attempts to walk forward I was gradually forced back. I felt some unseen, unknown power pushing against me and in the end I was compelled to turn around and leave the wood...' (quoted from Underwood's *This Haunted Isle*).

R. Thurston Hopkins, himself a writer of the supernatural, once led a ghost-hunting tour through the woods, and one of the group members claimed to have a run-in with the grotesque spectre of a decaying corpse - coughing, choking, and clutching at a throat that showed all too clearly the marks of hanging. Traumatised by what he had seen, the ghost hunter never knew how he managed to find his way back to the rest of the group.

Intrigued by what his companion had seen, Thurston Hopkins made some investigations and learned that a young farm labourer named David Leary had been hanged for the murder of a Mr Russell, with whom he had been lodging. The story was that Leary and Russell set out to steal some corn one evening, and that Russell suddenly collapsed and died holding the stolen booty. To hide their crime and to deflect suspicion from himself, Leary hid Russell's body in the woods. It was soon discovered, however, and an incompetent doctor claimed to find an incriminating amount of arsenic in the corpse.

Local tongues were wagging by this time, insisting that Leary had been having a clandestine affair with Mrs Russell, and that the two lovers had plotted the murder of her husband. Mrs Russell was imprisoned, but Leary was sentenced to death by hanging.

Before he was executed, Leary's last words to the chaplain were 'I beg of you to believe me when I say I am innocent, and to prove it I shall return to haunt those people who have hounded me to my death.'

Medical tests were later conducted, proving that Mr Russell had indeed died naturally, of a heart attack. His wife was released from prison, but it was too late to save David Leary, who apparently made good his promise to haunt Gladwish Wood.

Was the eerie sensation of evil that Rudyard Kipling felt there actually caused by the vengeful spirit of the hanged man? Kipling professed himself not to be psychic, and even expressed scepticism toward the paranormal. But he had a lifelong fascination with the subject, often featuring tales of the miraculous and the supernatural in his work, and by his own admission, he was 'sensitive' to things he couldn't see, hear, or touch.

Likewise, visitors to the idyllic Bateman's, whether they believe in ghosts or not, can't help but be aware of the spirit of the Kiplings - it remains alive and well in their beloved house in the Sussex Weald.

Battle Abbey
BATTLE, EAST SUSSEX

Battle Abbey, on the site of the Battle of Hastings, is probably the most haunted place in Sussex, if not in all of England. For it was here, on 14 October 1066 that William, Duke of Normandy, won the most significant battle in English history. By slaying King Harold and defeating his Saxon army, William brought Norman rule to England and so changed the course of events for all time.

On that momentous day, with probably around 14,000 soldiers engaged in combat, the number of men killed on both sides was terrible. In 1070, as a penance for the slaughter, the victorious William the Conqueror decreed that a Benedictine abbey should be built on the site, with the high altar of the church occupying the exact spot where his opponent King Harold had met his death. The construction of the church was completed by about 1094, and by the end of the century six years later, various other parts of the monastery had also been finished. Battle Abbey continued to grow in size and influence, and in 1338-39 the Great Gatehouse was built, ironically, as a defence against French raids. A few years afterwards, the Black Death killed many inhabitants of the Abbey, and the numbers continued to decline, in spite of some rebuilding in the fifteenth century.

But Battle Abbey's function as a monastery came to an end during the reign of Henry VIII. In 1538, during the Dissolution of the Monasteries, the king gave the Abbey and much of the land to Sir Anthony Browne, who immediately pulled down the church, chapter house, and part of the cloisters, using their stones as building materials for his other Sussex property, Cowdray House. In addition to other rebuilding work, Browne also transformed the Abbot's House into his own personal mansion.

The Brownes owned the Battle Abbey estate until 1715, when it was sold to Sir Thomas Webster. Except for the years between 1857-1901, the property remained in the Webster family until 1976. More demolition and rebuilding occurred in the eighteenth and nineteenth centuries, and after the First World War the mansion was leased to Battle Abbey School, an establishment for girls that is still there. Much of the building was ruined in a disastrous fire in 1931, but fortunately the most important parts were restored. In 1976 a donation from the United States saved the grounds for posterity, and now both the battlefield and the Abbey ruins are managed by English Heritage.

Some knowledge of the long history of Battle Abbey is helpful to an understanding of the many ghost stories that have originated there through the centuries. It would be interesting to know just how long after the Battle of Hastings the first tales were told. Did the newly victorious King William hear any of these, and if so, were they instrumental in any way in his decision to build an abbey on the site?

Some of the earliest stories undoubtedly concerned the battle itself, and even today there are tales that the fighting, or at least portions of it, are re-enacted on each anniversary, although most of these are considered to be apocryphal. A phantom man on horseback is said to ride across the battlefield every year, with some saying that he represents the first warrior to have been killed in the conflict. He is sometimes described as a white-bearded Saxon, or even a Druid! But others believe that this spectre might be that of Tallefer, the Norman troubadour who, some say, started the fighting by charging toward Saxon lines. According to R. Stevens-Bassett, Tallefer, singing a song of heroism, rode toward the enemy, stopping three times to throw his lance in the air and catch it by the point. Then he hurled the lance at a Saxon soldier and killed him. He repeated the same ritual with his sword before plunging into the lines, slicing and hacking at the soldiers around him. None of this may be historically accurate, Stevens-Bassett admits, but even so, every year the troubadour's ghost is said to gallop across the field as he makes his spectral charge (*Ghostly Tales & Hauntings of East Sussex*, CLX, 1993, 23).

The same author repeats the legend that the entire battle is re-enacted by the ghosts on the anniversary at midnight - surely a romantic touch, for if the battle were really played out anew every year, why wouldn't it be during the daytime, when it actually occurred? Naturally, the ghosts of both William the Conqueror and King Harold are said to walk or ride across the battlefield, both looking sorrowful. King Harold often appears with an arrow sticking out of his eye - this in spite of the fact that most historians no longer believe that this was how he died. Others claim that the battle has left aural as well as visual echoes - that the ghostly sounds of the fighting, as well as the cries of wounded and dying men, have been heard as far away as Pevensey Castle.

One of the most enduring myths from the battle is that even today, after a heavy rain, the ground at Battle Abbey runs red with blood. A similar legend states that a fountain of blood spurts upward from the spot where King Harold met his death (today, a small stone marker is all that is left to indicate the area). In spite of the prevalence of these tales, no one seems to believe them, although writers often remark that they may have started because of the existence of iron oxide in the soil.

Another of the most famous legends involves the curse pronounced on the family of Sir Anthony Browne, who was given Battle Abbey and much of the land around it by Henry VIII. Many versions of the story exist, but probably the best known is that Sir Anthony was cursed by one of the departing monks. (For a fuller discussion of the curse and its effect upon the Browne family, see the chapter on Cowdray House and Ruins in this book.) According to most chroniclers of the tale, the monk prophesied that Sir Anthony Browne's line should perish 'by fire and water', and it certainly did, although the curse took more than two hundred and fifty years to work. First, the Brownes' other ancestral home, Cowdray House, was almost totally destroyed in a fire in September 1793, and just a few days later, George Samuel Browne, the young heir, was himself drowned while attempting to navigate some waterfalls on the Rhine. Afterwards, the estate passed to George's sister Elizabeth, but her two sons also met their death by water, drowning in a boating accident at Bognor in 1815.

Some people believe that that wasn't the end of the curse - a fire in 1931 gutted the Abbot's House that Sir Anthony Browne had remodelled for his own use. According to a former pupil who attended the girls' school at the time, a small blaze broke out for the next two years on the anniversary of the first fire, until a member of the clergy was summoned in 1933 to lay the curse for all time (see http://groups.msn.com/BattleAbbeyReunionSite/ghouliesandghostiesnd.msnw).

The same pupil also recalled that two ghosts were said to walk the grounds of Battle Abbey during her time there. One was a man who went around with his head under his arm, and the other was a wailing woman who was occasionally seen ambling about.

Both of these phantoms might well have been products of the overactive imaginations of schoolgirls, but the same can't be said about the many tales of ghostly monks haunting Battle Abbey. In a 2003 broadcast of the television programme *Paranormal Files,* visitor operations team member Daryl Burchmore related that since arriving in 1990, he has heard a number of tales involving police officers who reported seeing the spectral monks during night-time stakeouts to catch vandals. The programme also included the story of a mother visiting the Abbey with her son and daughter. Both mother and son, but not the daughter, saw what they first assumed to be a costumed guide or actor dressed as a monk, only to be assured later that no such person was on the grounds.

R. Stevens-Bassett in his *Ghostly Tales & Hauntings of East Sussex* briefly mentions a monk who has been seen disappearing from the high street into the church wall (CLX, 1993). But in most of the other tales, the monk, often wearing a cowl, is said to walk near the aptly named Monk's Walk (or Wall, as it is also called). This ghost was reportedly witnessed on many occasions during the twentieth century, and when the nearby church was damaged by fire in 1931, he was seen several times on successive nights. His identity is unknown, although according to Rosemary Ellen Guiley, some believe him to be the monk who called down the curse on Sir Anthony Browne (*The Encyclopedia of Ghosts and Spirits*. New York: Facts On File, 1992, 34).

Reports of a phantom haunting Monk's Walk go back at least as far as the end of the nineteenth century. Lilian Boys Behrens's *Battle Abbey Under Thirty-Nine Kings* mentions that talk of the ghost at one time created such a commotion that locals decided to set a watch. One night as they waited silently, their efforts were rewarded. A figure in white appeared, walking slowly, seeming to be either deep in thought or in some kind of trance. But then one of the watchers noticed that this was no phantom monk or any other kind of supernatural being - this was a live, flesh-and-blood woman, the Duchess of Cleveland, experiencing an episode of sleepwalking (London: Saint Catherine Press, 1937, 125).

The Duchess of Cleveland lived at the Abbey for a time before her death in 1901. She was certainly no ghost then, but some say that she is now, and that it is her wraith, and not some spectral monk, who haunts the so-called Monk's Walk these days.

Whatever the identity of the phantom, reports of sightings continue. A custodian of Bayham Old Abbey, another haunted property, told me that a former resident of the tenant flat at Battle Abbey had once seen some kind of apparition moving along the path, although she had given him no further details. Ivor Noel Morgan White grew up in the Battle Abbey grounds, and on his delightful website devoted to all aspects of the place, he includes excerpts from a book by Peggie Phipps Boegner, whose grandparents leased the Abbey from the Webster family from 1894-1915. In Boegner's *Halcyon Days: an American Family Through Three Generations,* she remembers the legends of ghostly monks murdered by Thomas Cromwell's agents during the Dissolution of the Monasteries. On moonlit nights the phantom monks were said to stroll leisurely along the yew walk leading to the rose garden. 'We were in the habit of carrying salt in our pockets to ward off any spirit,' Boegner writes. 'If one threw salt and made the sign of the cross, any evil spirit would have to vanish!' (New York: Old Westbury Gardens and Abrams, 1986). (This quotation was taken from Ivor's website at http://www.battle-abbey.co.uk/album05.htm.)

Peggie Phipps Boegner's father, John Phipps, duplicated the rose gardens and ghost walk of Battle Abbey when he built Old Westbury Gardens in Long Island, New York, in the early 1900s. Constructed for his wife, Margarita Grace Phipps, the mansion was intended to resemble her childhood home at Battle Abbey. The story of the ghostly monks haunting the yew path at the Abbey is repeated in an article about Old Westbury Gardens - this time, however, the author mistakenly reports that the ghostly monks had been slain not by Cromwell's men but by soldiers of William the Conqueror! Obviously, there were yet to be either monks or a monastery at the site when the Battle of Hastings took place, but the author was probably just repeating the version of the legend as she heard it from her interview subject (Lyn Dobrin, 'Old Westbury Gardens - Long Island, New York,' *Flower & Garden Magazine*, March 2001, reprinted at http://www.findarticles.com/p/articles/mi_m1082/is_2_45/ai_72274511).

Still more authors have written about ghostly monks who pop up at various locations around Battle Abbey. Andrew Green in *Haunted Sussex Today* describes the eerie experience of a couple in February 1996. The husband was a falconer, demonstrating hunting techniques with birds of prey in the open ruins of the reredorter, the Abbey's former latrine block that adjoins the fishponds and the Common House. The man was astonished to see the phantom of a monk in a black habit walk toward part of the Guest House and then vanish into thin air. The falconer's wife also saw the figure and was said to be 'a little affected by her experience' (Seaford, East Sussex: S.B. Publications, 1997, 12-14, 87).

Green also tells about the haunting experienced a few years before this by James Minahane and his mother, who visited Battle Abbey on a hot sunny day in August. James, noticing a walk bordered by yew trees along a high boundary wall, left his mother waiting while he went to see where it led. Even though the weather was hot, James felt a sudden chill halfway down the path. He saw that the walk had a dead end, so he returned to his mother standing on the lawn. With a shocked expression on her face, she asked him what had happened to the other people who had been on the path with him. James replied that he had been alone, but his mother insisted that she had seen two monks, one in an off-white or butter-coloured habit, and the other in black. No cowls were visible, but both men were wearing sandals. The monks had a benign appearance and looked to be in their thirties. The one in the off-white habit was short and heavy with long ginger hair, and the monk dressed in black had dark hair and a pale complexion. They were solid-looking figures with nothing hazy about them, and they seemed to be arguing, waving their arms as if to emphasise various points. They walked to the end of the path, where they suddenly vanished.

James and his mother were so intrigued by their unprecedented experience that they carried out some research. They discovered that the path James had been walking on was called the 'Monks Walk' on one old map and the 'Ghosts Walk' on another. The monk in black had been dressed in the habit of the Benedictines, an order vowed to silence, and the other might have been a

Cistercian, possibly from the abbey founded at Robertsbridge in 1250 by an Abbot from Battle, Robert de St Martin. This was the first Cistercian abbey in the country, and its monks wore habits of rough sheepskin or lamb's wool, which would have been off-white in colour.

The figure of an elderly man who appeared in 1974 in the Common House might also have been a phantom monk. In *Ghosts of Today* Andrew Green writes of a tourist who asked one of the guides about the man's identity, only to be assured that she was the only one who could see him. The woman said that the ghost seemed to be wearing a brown leather jerkin and apron, symbols of a farrier, but more recent sightings indicate that the figure might actually be a monk wearing a brown habit. The female tourist who witnessed him was so distressed by her experience that she had to be treated for mild shock (London: Kaye & Ward, 1980, 31-32).

Green believes that this might be the same apparition seen by Joyce Pain, who was walking along the pavement beside the churchyard at St Mary's Parish Church one evening. As she drew near to the solicitor's office, she realised that a monk in a dark habit with his face hidden by the cowl was gliding along the pavement towards the gateway of Battle Abbey. Joyce watched him walk for about ten yards before he suddenly vanished. She claimed to feel no fear, only astonishment at having seen a ghost.

One of the most startling sightings of a ghostly monk occurred in January 1982. Andrew Green tells the tale in *Haunted Sussex Today*, but I received an even fuller account from Daryl Burchmore. A maintenance man working for the Ministry of Public Works was crouching down to do some work in the Guest House. He called out to a colleague to pass him a tool, but when he got no response, he looked up to find the unexpected figure of a black-clad monk peering over him. As the astounded workman watched, the monk slowly faded from view.

'The workman was absolutely terrified and he wouldn't go back inside that building for years,' Daryl told me. 'Numbers of people have said that they've had weird experiences in that particular place. It is creepy. On the other side of it is what we call the stone store, where we keep various bits of masonry. The other day I went in to lock up, and I found the door broken open. Someone had obviously gone in there. I put my head round the corner, but then thought, no, I'm not going in. It just felt weird.'

Green's account goes on to say that a few years after the maintenance man had his scare, a custodian was checking the same building when he twice heard the sound of a man's voice yelling 'Let me out'. The custodian searched the premises but could find no explanation for the voice.

On 30 April 2002, teacher Jill Sutcliffe of Sutton Valence Prep School near Maidstone in Kent had an especially intriguing encounter in this same area. 'We were on a school trip,' Jill told me, 'and I was walking with two boys, nine years old. We were following the class, bringing up the rear. It was a nasty, windy day, and we were splattered by rain. As we walked past the open door of the store room, or undercroft, we saw a monk.

'He was walking towards us, along what looked like a passageway, and then he turned right before he reached the doorway,' Jill recalled. 'He turned right and then went through another doorway. We looked at him, all three of us, and carried on walking. I said to the boys, "It would have been nice to have had a chat to him, and find out what he's doing today." He was indoors and dry, and we were outside, wet and miserable.

'He looked very real - I felt that I could have spoken to him and he would have talked to me. He looked just like any other chap, and because there's a school at Battle Abbey, I thought that he might have been a chaplain there. But later on, when I mentioned him to other members of our school, everyone wondered what I was talking about. When I mentioned it at the shop, someone said, "It's so unfair - the visitors always see him, but we don't!" That's when we found out that a ghostly monk has been seen at that spot several times over the years.'

'I don't really believe in ghosts,' Jill insisted. 'If you wanted to tell me that this sighting was a hoax and that someone was actually dressing up as a monk that day, I would believe you, because he seemed so real.'

Jill recalls that the monk seemed not to notice her or the boys, and just went on about his business. He was chubby and looked as if he were in his late 60s, dressed in a creamy white habit with a red belt and brown sandals. His hair was grey with a monk's tonsure.

'I taught in a Catholic order years ago, and I'm used to brothers,' she assured me. 'I remember the way they seemed to float with their long robes hanging behind them, and that's what this monk looked like. I can see that robe moving now.'

Jill returned on another occasion to the spot, and upon walking into the store room, she noticed that she could see no doorway where there had been one before. 'I've been back twice since then for the same school outing,' she said. 'Once when I looked into the room, the children were inside and I couldn't see them at all well. I don't understand how the light worked that day when we saw the monk, especially as the weather then was dark and miserable. But for some reason we were able to see him very clearly.'

The two students who saw the monk at the same time as Jill returned to the school to write down what they had seen and to draw a picture. That the boys also saw the apparition reassures Jill, as does the fact that another monk, or perhaps the same one in different coloured clothing, was seen just a few weeks later by the mother and son mentioned earlier in this chapter. All their accounts appeared on the television programme *Paranormal Files.*

'The mother and son saw a monk wearing a woolly brown habit,' Jill explained, 'but ours was definitely wearing creamy white. I was a bit surprised at that, because from what I've read, I thought that monks wore woolly, heavy habits. I mentioned that to people at the shop, and someone explained that perhaps ours was wearing a ceremonial habit. Those were white, so maybe something special was happening that day that the monk was celebrating.'

'I don't know how you explain these things,' Jill continued. 'I kept thinking that someone was hoaxing us. Also, if what we saw was a figment of our imaginations, we really should have seen a Norman soldier or King Harold, because we had been talking about 1066 and that's why we were there.'

Indeed, an armour-clad medieval knight, carrying a sword, has been sighted in another part of the Abbey, in a corner of the ruined Great Hall. Andrew Green gives accounts of the ghostly knight in three of his books: *Our Haunted Kingdom* (Fontana/Collins, 1973, 285-86); *Ghosts of Today;* and *Haunted Sussex Today.* In the first book, Green says that the knight was seen one afternoon in June 1971 by a young boy 'cradled in the arms of his father'. Startled by the appearance of the apparition, the child suddenly cried out, 'Who is that man over there, Daddy, the one with the long sword?' The boy was the only one in the area who could see the apparition, although one or two of the others claimed to feel a presence. The young guide conducting tours at the time believed that the child's sighting of the ghost was genuine, as he had been staring into a corner of the room for some time, and his description of the phantom tallied with those who had seen the apparition previously. Besides that, the guide added, the subject of ghosts had not been mentioned, so the child's imagination could not have been stirred in that way.

In a later book, *Ghosts of Today,* Green mentions only that a Norman knight was seen by a 'young boy', but this time the event is said to have occurred in 1972. The one-year discrepancy is probably accounted for by nothing more than a typographical error, but in his *Haunted Sussex Today,* published over a decade later, Green writes that the knight was witnessed by a 'fourteen-year-old Canadian boy on his first trip to England in 1972'.

Does this latter account refer to a completely separate sighting of the ghost, or did Green receive conflicting information about the earlier story when he updated research for the later book? Andrew Green himself unfortunately died in May 2004, so we may never know for sure.

Several female ghosts have also been reported at Battle Abbey, by Green as well as by other writers. In *Ghosts of Today,* he writes that Joyce Pain, mentioned earlier, not only saw a phantom monk but also had a mystifying experience when she became secretary to the headmistress of the school in the Abbot's House. One day when she was halfway up the main staircase in the Great Hall, she was startled to hear a loud rustling sound like that made by someone wearing a silk skirt. No one else was present, and Joyce checked all around her, even walking into the alcove at the bend of the stairs and into the staff room at the end of the corridor. Nothing could account for the sound. When Joyce later admitted what she had heard, she learned that footsteps, associated with a mysterious lady in red, had been heard previously on the same stairs.

In the late 1970s another (or perhaps the same?) red-clad phantom was seen by Marcus Granger, one of a group of visitors being conducted around the Abbey. Green reports in both *Ghosts of Today* and *Haunted Sussex Today* that the figure of a woman in a long red gown of the Elizabethan period suddenly appeared in the top western corner of the Great Hall, the same place where the ghostly knight and the farrier or brown monk have been sighted at other times. According to Granger, however, this phantom's dress seemed to be made of velvet rather than silk.

A less glamorous ghost, a limping lady in grey, is believed to walk along the corridor leading from the Great Hall to the Abbot's House. Andrew Green writes in *Ghosts of Today* that a student heard the heavy limping footsteps at around 9.30 one night in September 1974. At that time, they seemed to be proceeding down the passageway towards the Hall.

Ivor Noel Morgan White, whose grandfather, father, and brother all worked as kitchen gardeners at Battle Abbey, recalls some strange tales he heard there as a child. 'My grandad, Walter White, told us of the lady in a long white cloak who would appear walking along the path which is now known as "Camelia Walk",' Ivor told me. 'It runs along the main wall separating the Abbey from St Mary's Church on the other side of Upper Lake. He claimed to have seen this ghost, and as a child, I really believed him.'

The phantom Walter White claimed to see was none other than that of the Duchess of Cleveland, whose sleepwalking exploits had led villagers to believe she was a ghost long before her death in 1901! In the late 1920s, Walter White told his grandson about having seen the ghost of the Duchess just a few years previously, in the early 1920s.

'As far as I can remember, he told me that she was wearing a long white gown which came down to her ankles,' Ivor continued. 'And she walked from the front of the Abbey down toward my grandfather's walled garden. He was Head Gardener, and he raised fruits and vegetables. There was also a conservatory where he raised exotic tropical plants.'

'He claimed that the ghost followed him in to the conservatory and gave him advice about pruning the grapes,' Ivor said. 'The Duchess of Cleveland had been an expert gardener. You have to prune grapes in a certain way so as to encourage them to grow large without leaving too many on one stem. She would direct him as to which buds to cut off so as to leave the best ones to produce the grapes. My grandfather was a regular prize-winner at all the local flower shows, especially with his exotic fruits. My father also worked as a gardener there, and he saw the ghost as well. But I don't think she actually spoke to him.'

Ivor is certain that his grandfather could not have been influenced by Lilian Boys Behrens's *Battle Abbey Under Thirty-Nine Kings* when he related his tales, as the book was not published until 1937. 'The author suggests that it wasn't actually a ghost that the villagers of Battle saw, but the sleepwalking Duchess of Cleveland,' Ivor said. 'But what my grandfather saw must have been a ghost, the ghost of the duchess. He had actually known her while she was alive, and when he heard her voice in the conservatory, he immediately recognised it. So he put two and two together and realised that he was seeing her ghost.'

Walter White, 1868-1942. Head Gardener at Battle Abbey, he reportedly enjoyed a friendly relationship with the ghost of the Duchess of Cleveland.
Photo courtesy of Ivor Noel Morgan White.

Ivor has nevertheless wondered about whether the account in the book is true, as well as whether 'Grandad Wally' was telling fibs. 'I leave you to decide,' he told me.

Whether the Duchess of Cleveland returned to advise Ivor's grandfather about grape pruning or not, it's clear that she wasn't the elderly female phantom who terrorised Lady Webster. Victorian writer Augustus Hare tells of the spectre witnessed by this lady, who had come to stay at Battle Abbey not long after her marriage. As she was lying in bed one night, the bedcurtains were suddenly drawn apart to reveal the terrifying phantom of an old woman. The phantom stared at Lady Webster for a few moments before walking away and going out through the door. She had appeared completely solid, so much so that Lady Webster had believed her to be an old family retainer. No sooner had the ghost left than Lord Webster came into the room, to be completely astonished by his wife's question as to the woman's identity. He had seen no one in the corridor outside, he assured her, and if the woman had been real, he would have passed her just outside the door.

A much younger ghost, a phantom girl, has been reported at Pyke House, a residential training centre adjoining the site of Battle Abbey. Andrew Green in *Ghosts of Today* reports that the warden, a Mr Hobson, claimed that the spectre had been witnessed 'on quite a few occasions', hurrying along an upstairs corridor near his flat and 'gliding through a bedroom' before disappearing when she got to the window. Believed to be the daughter of a nineteenth-century owner of the building, the ghost seemed to be wearing a long white dress resembling a nightgown. The story is that she suffered a tragic love affair and killed herself by jumping into a lake in the field behind the house. Green claims that on several occasions the phantom's wispy shape has been seen moving through the back garden towards a large pool, where she then vanishes (47-48).

Another phantom that might be expected to haunt similar watery areas is that of a white swan, mentioned in passing by Peggie Phipps Boegner in her *Halcyon Days: an American Family Through Three Generations*. But instead of making its presence known in a sensible location such as a lake, this eerie creature used to appear in one of the spare rooms at the Abbey!

Not all the Battle Abbey supernatural phenomena are of the visual kind. A man calling himself 'Mark' who is involved in medieval re-enactment left an unusual story on a website (http://thesupernaturalworld.co.uk/forum/index.php?s=290390b9cbb0e9ef586464b787c3fac3&showtopic=194). His re-enactment group was visiting Battle Abbey a few years ago, and one evening after enjoying a few pints, Mark, along with two men and three women, were walking through the grounds. The women moved off into the darkness across the school gardens. The men continued wandering along the walls, when they heard a scream and saw their three female companions running out of the Guest House, shaken and pale.

They told the men that they had gone into the large room, planning to jump out and scare them when they came to find them. Two women, a mother and daughter, had stood to the right of the door, and one woman had stood to its left. As they heard the men approaching on the gravel path, they prepared to lunge out at them. But the woman standing at the left of the door suddenly felt a hand pushing her hard, towards the doorway. The other two felt a cold breeze across the backs of their necks and heard from behind what sounded like 'an angry exhalation'. All three ran as fast as they could to escape.

'We searched every corner with our torch expecting to find a drunk re-enactor laughing himself silly, but [found] nothing,' Mark writes, adding that the men were pleased that the 'ghost' had turned the ladies' joke against them. They were, however, genuinely worried by the fear on the women's faces.

In the summer of 1990, Daryl Burchmore had a similarly disquieting experience during his first season at the Abbey. 'It was around six o'clock one evening, and I went round to lock the undercroft, the series of wine cellars that are part of the former Guest Range,' Daryl told me. 'It's probably the eeriest place on site, not somewhere you like going on your own. It's so creepy that it was going to be used in an episode of *Doctor Who* a few years ago.'

'That night I had a sense of someone watching me as I locked up,' Daryl continued. 'When I came to a chamber door, I locked up the three shutters, one for the window and two for the main door. Suddenly there was this huge "Bang bang bang" from inside as if someone were saying "Let me out!" The only people I could see were far away, out on the battlefield. Admittedly, people could climb in through the open window nearby, but I would have heard them scrambling up.'

'I went running back to the shop, and my colleague thought I was joking,' Daryl continued. 'Then he saw my face and said, "No, you're not!" Later that night a team of my colleagues went round to the undercroft and used divining rods that kept pointing over to a particular corner.'

A few years later, around February 1998, the Sussex Southern Research group also heard the loud banging noise. Paul Holloway was one of the paranormal investigation team members who were standing and chatting outside a large door to one of the rooms in the undercroft. 'Just out of nowhere there was an almighty single crashing thud on the timber door,' Paul told me. 'It wasn't that anything had fallen over. This was a very aggressive, "I'm here" type of thing. Even our sceptic, a photographer, said it was the only thing he couldn't explain. That was the loudest knock we've ever heard in ten or twelve years.'

Paul added that several times, usually in the early evening, the group has heard footsteps crunching along a nearby gravel path when there was no one else about. They have also heard unexplained voices in one of the top rooms.

But Innes Jones of St Asaph in Denbighshire has had probably the oddest experience involving unexplained aural phenomena at Battle Abbey. Around five o'clock on the sunny, clear Friday afternoon of 11 June 2004, she and a friend had just finished listening to their audio tours of the grounds.

'We had nearly completed our tour,' Innes told me. 'We were near the area where the icehouse was, when suddenly I heard music. I thought I'd forgotten to switch off my audio device, but I checked and saw that it was turned off.'

Innes's next thought was that the Battle Abbey staff might have been playing a tape of music to help create an atmosphere of authenticity. 'I looked around and couldn't see where the music was coming from, but I could still hear it,' she insisted. 'It was beautiful abbey music, like nuns singing, very soft but so clear and very tuneful. If I heard it again, I would recognize it, although I didn't know the tune. It sounded as though it was coming from some walls close by, or perhaps from behind them.'

'I shouted to my friend, "Do you hear music?" She walked towards me, and when she was about two or three paces away, the singing stopped.' Neither her friend nor anyone else had heard the music, but Innes mentioned what had happened when she handed in her audio equipment. The staff member on duty assured her that no music was playing, but added that other odd occurrences had happened near the icehouse at a similar time of day.

Innes had never had an experience like this before, and still can't explain what she heard. All she knows is that she didn't imagine the singing - it was real, and she would love to have an explanation. Another thing that puzzles her is that it was clearly women's voices that she heard, instead of those of male monks, who were known to have lived at the Abbey.

How, too, does one explain the photos with weird, inexplicable features that have been taken there? The front cover of Andrew Green's *Haunted Sussex Today* is illustrated with a photo taken by a Mr Lovett-Darby in 1974. Green explains that when the photographer snapped a picture of his daughter in the ruins of the Common Room, no one else was about. But the developed photo clearly shows a very solid-looking figure in the arched doorway. The apparition looks like a man, wearing what seems to be a white or pale-coloured knee-length tunic over loose-fitting trousers of the same colour. The tunic seems to be drawn in or belted at the waist with a dark band or belt. The head of the figure is barely visible, as it is in darkness; whereas from the neck down, the apparition seems to be standing in light projected from above and to the side.

In the same book, Green mentions a photo taken in June 1996 by Stewart Dunkley from Zimbabwe. The photo was taken of the side of one of the buildings in the Abbey ruins, and an automatic camera was used to exclude the risk of double exposure. The resulting print shows a beam of light beside a chimney stack, and on taking a close look at the photo, one of the custodians claimed that he could make out the face of a man.

Daryl Burchmore told me of a previously unpublished and now misplaced photo taken by a visitor of the Old Town hanging post underneath the Gatehouse. This one, taken from a distance, shows a shaft of light behind the post. On closer inspection, however, the shaft of light is said to resemble a dangling, hanged corpse.

Stacey and Stuart Logan's Children of the City (COTC) Paranormal Investigations discovered a plethora of odd phenomena when they went to explore Battle Abbey. Some of the group experienced a strange sense of foreboding and the feeling of a drop in temperature within a clump of trees near the battlefield. And like Daryl Burchmore and Paul Holloway, several of them heard an unexplained knocking sound coming from the walls of the renowned undercroft where so many strange things have occurred. Photos taken there revealed the presence of 'ectoplasmic mists' and mysterious balls of light, or orbs, believed by many investigators to be early or primitive manifestations of apparitions. Another orb was sighted in the Novice Chamber of the chapel (for photos and more investigation reports see the COTC website at www.cotcpi.co.uk).

Independent investigator Stuart Mintram has long had an interest in paranormal photography, and he captured some of these orbs with his digital camera just before Christmas 2003. 'I went into the chapel area and felt as if something was looking down on me from the ceiling,' he told me. 'It was a really nasty feeling, and I had to walk out of there pretty fast. But a few days later I conquered my fear and went back to take photos of the hearth area. I took three pictures, one after the other, and in each of them, there are orbs flying everywhere. I just took the photos on the off chance that I might get something unusual, because I did sense something there.'

Stuart had never before managed to capture anything unusual with his camera, and he saw nothing out of the ordinary when he took the photos. 'But I've always sensed something in that room,' he explained, 'and I believe that there was some kind of spiritual action there before I arrived. Maybe someone had passed on from that room and left energy behind. I go back often now because I want to see whether it's there all the time.'

Because of all the accounts of supernatural phenomena at Battle Abbey, it seems likely that this leftover energy is indeed present much of the time. Many living souls besides Stuart Mintram have felt it, and many understand all too well the sensation described by John Burke in his book, *Sussex* (London: B.T. Batsford Ltd, 1974, 44): 'I have, however, found myself shivering uncontrollably, even in bright sunshine, when passing one steep cleft below the battlefield - perhaps the ditch, running red with blood, in which took place the final slaughter.'

A single orb in the chapel of Battle Abbey.
Photo courtesy of Stuart Mintram.

More orbs appear in the chapel of Battle Abbey.
Photo courtesy of Stuart Mintram.

Stuart Mintram's final shot of the orbs in the chapel of Battle Abbey. At the time these photos were taken, one after the other, Stuart saw nothing unusual but sensed some kind of presence in the chapel.
Photo courtesy of Stuart Mintram.

Bayham Abbey

ON THE SUSSEX/KENT BORDER, NEAR LAMBERHURST, KENT

The peaceful, picturesque ruins of Bayham Abbey lie on the border between Sussex and Kent. Built in the early thirteenth century, the Abbey was home to Premonstratensian monks whose phantoms, according to legend, continue to frequent the spot. Dressed in white robes, chanting, and winding their way around what remains of the Abbey, the ghostly canons are reportedly accompanied by the pealing of bells and the fragrance of burning incense. Most accounts agree that the eerie procession is generally seen on moonlit nights around midnight, but another version claims that it occurs shortly before dusk. Some visitors to the ruins claim to have watched the monks for as long as a few minutes before they disappeared into the shadows.

At least two visitors to Bayham Abbey have reported another strange occurrence there, but this one might turn out not to have a supernatural cause. Paul Holloway, a Southern Ghost Research member based in Eastbourne, recalled one trip to the ruins on a Sunday morning in June or July of 1999. He and a friend believed themselves to be the only ones there, yet around 11.30 or 12 o'clock they distinctly heard the voices of what they took to be a young girl and boy, aged about five or six.

'We couldn't see anyone, and we couldn't hear what they were saying, as they were mumbling,' Paul told me. 'But they sounded as if they were forty or fifty feet away. The voices went on for several minutes.'

Although Paul and his friend couldn't see anyone else in the vicinity of the old ruins, and wondered whether they were hearing something otherworldly, a long-time caretaker of Bayham Abbey offered a more down-to-earth explanation.

'I've been here since 1984, and I've never experienced anything unusual,' he said. 'There are four young children living right across the riverbank, and they can often be heard without being seen.'

But fortunately, as there are no longer any monks living anywhere near Bayham Abbey, the tales of their ghostly procession can't be so easily discounted!

Bodiam Castle
NEAR ROBERTSBRIDGE, EAST SUSSEX

odiam is everyone's ideal of what a castle should be. Surrounded by a moat and with its exterior virtually intact after more than six hundred years, Bodiam Castle looks as if it came from a fairy tale. Sir Edward Dalyngrigge received permission in 1385 to fortify his manor house in preparation for an invasion by French marauders. Mercifully, they never arrived, and Bodiam Castle was spared.

Historians squabble over just who may or may not have attacked Bodiam over the next few centuries, but everyone agrees that the chief enemy of the castle was time itself. By the nineteenth century the once proud building had fallen into serious dereliction and would have been demolished for scrap if the eccentric 'Mad Jack' Fuller of Brightling, MP for East Sussex, had not bought it to restore. Bodiam was sold again in 1864 to Lord Ashcombe, who continued the repairs, and for the last time, in 1916, to Lord Curzon. Curzon carried on the restoration work of his predecessors and willed the castle to the National Trust upon his death in 1925.

Only a few spooky stories involve Bodiam Castle, and details are scanty even about those. Probably the best known is that of the Lady in Red, a mysterious phantom who has appeared more than once on moonlit nights. She stands at the top of a tower, watching and waiting for an unknown someone. Another unidentified ghost is that of a young boy dressed in what appears to be nineteenth-century clothing. According to Andrew Green's *Haunted Sussex Today*, this apparition was seen most recently in 1994 by a castle custodian who was locking up the museum area (Seaford, East Sussex: S.B. Publications, 1997, 19). The phantom child was seen on the bridge, running toward the castle, only to vanish halfway across. One possible interpretation is that he fell into the moat and drowned.

Esther Meynell's *Small Talk in Sussex* describes a visitor who, upon entering the castle courtyard alone 'did not behold the empty shell we now see, but had a momentary vision of something happening there which so horrified him that he could never bear to speak of it' (London: Robert Hale & Company, 1954, 131).

Whatever terrible events may (or may not) have troubled Bodiam in the past, current property manager George Bailey claims to enjoy 'unrivalled peace' at the castle nowadays. But even he admits that there is something strange about the acoustic qualities in the area.

'We have heard what we thought were parties down by the pub half a mile away,' he told me, 'but when we checked, we discovered that what we were actually hearing was the bleating of sheep, three miles down the valley at Newenden!' Another example of sound distortion occurs during summer concerts at the castle, attended by upwards of two thousand people. 'We never hear a complaint from the adjacent village,' George insisted, 'but we regularly get comments about the noise volume from a village three miles away.'

George claims that the strange acoustic quality is present most of the time, and well known to at least three generations of area residents. Could it then help to provide an explanation for old tales of ghostly music, words spoken in an unknown tongue, and sounds of revelry coming from the castle precincts?

Peter Underwood explores the theme of mysterious sounds at Bodiam in *This Haunted Isle: The Ghosts and Legends of Britain's Historic Buildings* (Poole, New York, Sidney: Javelin Books, 1986, 32-33). He recalled a lecture to the Ghost Club given in the 1920s by noted psychic researcher and investigator Harry Price.

'Of Bodiam Castle he said he had traced stories of the sounds of revelry at night, at certain times during the winter months, the sound emanating quite distinctly from within the shell of the castle,' Underwood writes. He then quotes Price further, saying that the 'clanking of drinking cups, songs in a foreign tongue, intermixed with strange oaths, have been heard over and over again by people passing the ruins late at night.' Another strange feature of the haunting was the music, 'faint but distinct', which 'can always be heard on Easter Sunday by those whose ears are attuned to "psychic music"'.

Were these sounds phantom echoes from the castle's past or merely the everyday noises from pubs and churches, broadcast by the odd acoustics of the valley to mystified listeners miles away?

Bramber Castle

BRAMBER, WEST SUSSEX

esides some few and ragged ruins, the ghostly legends are about all that remain of the once-great Bramber Castle, built by William de Braose shortly after the Battle of Hastings to guard what used to be a busy port on the river Adur. The name 'Bramber', taken from the Saxon 'Brymmburh', meant 'fortified place', and until its destruction by Parliamentary forces in the Civil War, the castle lived up to its name. The only physical remainders of the castle are a part of the keep, portions of the curtain wall, and a pre-Conquest motte found within the walls.

The most famous story of the supernatural at Bramber Castle begins with the great grandson of the builder, also named William de Braose. This William married Maud (also known as Matilda) de St Valery at some time before 1170. Upon their marriage, the couple inherited from William's family vast amounts of property in Wales, where they went to live at Abergavenny Castle.

In 1176, William gained a reputation as a murderous traitor when he invited many of the most prominent men in Wales to a feast, only to slaughter them in revenge for the death of his uncle, Henry of Hereford. Sitsylt ap Dimswald was one of the unlucky guests, and when William had finished killing him, he went to his house to slay the man's son in front of the mother. For a grand finale, he set the house on fire.

Feeling remorseful afterwards, William tried to make restitution by building a church at New Shoreham in Sussex and conferring large endowments on churches in Normandy and Wales. He and Maud then tried to settle down with their family at Bramber, but fresh troubles with King John loomed on the horizon.

Barons such as William were already resisting the king's tyrannical rule, and in 1215 they would force him to put his seal on the Magna Charta. But in the years preceding that, in order to subdue the growing disloyalty from the barons, John began demanding hostages from them. When the king's messengers demanded that William and Maud hand over their sons, the defiant Maud refused and spat out an insult. Certainly she would not hand over her sons to John, she insisted, as he had murdered his own nephew, Arthur, who was supposed to be under the king's protection.

Such a deadly accusation would ultimately seal the fate of Maud as well as that of her son William. Wanting revenge, the king called in a debt William owed, but he refused to pay. John then confiscated some of William's lands and demanded three of his grandsons, William, Philip, and Giles, as hostages until the payment was made.

Now William had no choice but to agree to the king's demands, but in addition, he plotted rebellion with his sons Reginald and William. The de Braoses tried to recover some of their lost castles but failed, so they attacked Leominster instead, burning and pillaging as they went. King John dispossessed and outlawed William in 1208.

Maud realised by this time that perhaps the family had gone too far in its feud with the king, so she sent peace offerings to him, among them a herd of four hundred cows and a bull. But the de Braoses, with their family, were nevertheless forced to flee to Ireland, and their lands were seized by the Crown.

In the meantime, new troubles with the king broke out in Wales, so William travelled there to join the fight. Maud and her children were besieged in Ireland but escaped and headed for Scotland, only to be captured at Galloway and handed over to the king. Enraged, John locked Maud and her son William in a dungeon at Windsor Castle.

Maud's husband William escaped from the king's pursuers by disguising himself as a beggar and fleeing to France. Once he got to Paris, he lost no time in telling King Philip about King John's murder of his nephew Arthur. In a drunken fury, William explained, the king killed the prince with his own hands and then threw the body into the River Seine.

William died in exile in France in 1211, but his wife Maud and their son William had starved to death at Windsor Castle the year before. Some say that when the bodies were recovered, it first appeared that Maud had died while clutching her son toward her for a final kiss. Upon closer inspection, however, it came clear that the starving woman had been gnawing at her son's emaciated cheek.

Whether this grisly detail is true or not, it is a fact that during her lifetime Maud was considered to be a formidable woman, even a warrior, as she had defended Pains Castle from a Welsh siege in 1198, earning it the name 'Matilda's Castle'. The Welsh even seemed to believe that she had supernatural powers, nicknaming her 'Moll Walbee' and 'the Lady of la Haie'. She was said to have built Hay Castle all by herself in the course of one night, carrying the stones in her apron. When one fell out and into her shoe, the legend tells us, the powerful Maud picked it up and flung it three miles away, across the River Wye, where it landed in St Meilig's churchyard. This nine-foot-high standing stone may still be seen inside the church.

But back at Maud's home at Bramber Castle, the terrible suffering of her family lives on in the form of another legend with several different versions. Writers repeating the tale have variously reported that two, three, or even four child phantoms have been seen, either at the castle or on the streets of Bramber, looking ragged, emaciated, and begging for food. All the chroniclers agree that the tragic spectres appear in the month of December, but some go further to say that the haunting takes place specifically during the Christmas season, or even on Christmas Day itself. All agree that regardless of their number, the small ghosts are indeed the de Braose children who starved to death with their mother (some say with their father, too) in the dungeon at Windsor Castle (some say at Corfe Castle). If anyone approaches them, they disappear. These apparitions have apparently not been witnessed for many years, however, perhaps not since the Victorian era. (For a reliable discussion of the de Braose family, their troubles with King John, and the ghost story, see the website of professional medieval genealogist Doug Thompson at http://freespace.virgin.net/doug.thompson/BraoseWeb/index1.htm.)

The second most famous tale of the supernatural at Bramber Castle involves another Maud, this time the young Maud of Ditchling, wife of the much older Lord Hubert de Hurst. At some time near the end of the fifteenth century, so the story goes, Lord Hubert discovered his wife in the arms of her lover, William de Lindfield. The insanely jealous and vengeful Lord Hubert had William imprisoned in the dungeon and fed him just enough each day to keep him alive. Lady Maud, agonising over her lover, had no idea where he was, and found him just in time to see the last bricks being laid in place to wall him up alive.

Some say that the cruel Lord Hubert forced Maud to hear the last moans of her dying lover before she herself died of a broken heart the next day. According to some versions of the tale, Lord Hubert died at the same time, nothing more than a raving maniac. When Bramber Castle was attacked by Parliamentarian troops in the seventeenth century, they were said to have discovered William de Lindfield's skeleton crouched in a corner, his head resting on his hands and his elbows on his knees.

According to Peter Underwood's *This Haunted Isle: The Ghosts and Legends of Britain's Historic Buildings,* a group of Bramber residents in 1954 reported hearing the sound of a woman wailing among the castle ruins, her cry consisting of four notes. They believed that what they were hearing was Lady Maud sobbing for her lost lover (Poole, New York, Sidney: Javelin Books, 1986, 33-4).

It's tempting to try to link the tragic tale of Lady Maud and William de Lindfield with a story told by 'a certain old man just before he died', related by Tony Wales in *The West Sussex Village Book* (Newbury, Berkshire: Countryside Books, 1994 (reprint) 34-5). When the man was a boy, he had entered a tunnel connected to the castle, but for some reason became frightened and was forced to turn back.

In the same entry, Wales reports another local legend, that of a ghostly white horse Bramber residents have apparently seen galloping around the dried-up moat of the castle on moonlit nights. According to Wales, one man even claimed that 'we 'ears 'is 'oofs, too'.

It's hard to say whether any of these legendary phantoms can be found at Bramber Castle nowadays. Indeed, when members of COTC Paranormal Investigations went to the area, they had no encounters with ghosts, but they did sense a feeling of despair in the north-eastern part of the site. And on their website, they include a photograph taken 'outside of our investigation' that they believe clearly shows 'some kind of strange ectoplasmic mist' on the left-hand side of the picture (http://www.cotcpi.co.uk/bramber%20castle%20report.htm).

Whether ghostly echoes remain or not at these forlorn but lovely ruins, Bramber Castle, managed by English Heritage, is the perfect spot to go to escape the present and to feel the poignant weight of past centuries.

Charleston Farmhouse

Near Firle, East Sussex

Charleston Farmhouse, country retreat of the Bloomsbury circle, still seems bursting with the exuberant personalities of those who made it such an individualistic expression of their lives and art. In 1916 artists Vanessa Bell and Duncan Grant came to live at Charleston, and they soon welcomed other members of the group who came to visit or reside there from time to time. They embellished the walls, doors, furniture and even ceramics with their own fantastic designs, transforming the simple farmhouse into a one-of-a kind domestic monument to creativity, as well as a haven for some of the leading intellectuals of the early twentieth century.

Perhaps that's why so many visitors and some of the staff have claimed to feel a strong presence at Charleston Farmhouse, as if members of the Bloomsbury group have just stepped out and might be returning at any moment. One person in a tour group claimed to have seen a ghost, but most simply report feeling a kind of spiritual presence.

Current staff members tend to dismiss the possibility of the supernatural at Charleston Farmhouse as a joke, taking most such stories with a big pinch of salt. Yet even they don't deny that because the Bloomsbury circle left such an indelible impression on the house, their spirit lives on.

Cowdray House
AND PARK RUINS, MIDHURST, WEST SUSSEX

f ever a place looked like the setting for a Gothic novel, Cowdray House and Park Ruins in Midhurst does. Indeed, its eerily beautiful appearance, along with the legend of its curse, led to Cowdray's being used as part of the setting for Anya Seton's *Green Darkness,* one of the best-loved historical romances of all time.

The name 'Cowdray' is believed to derive from the old French 'coudraie', meaning a hazel wood. Sir David Owen began building Cowdray in the early sixteenth century, and the Earl of Southampton continued its construction during the reign of Henry VIII. At the Dissolution of the Monasteries, the king granted Battle Abbey and its holdings to the earl's half brother, Sir Anthony Browne. When the earl died childless at about the same time, Sir Anthony also became owner of the Cowdray estate, and he razed some of the buildings at Battle Abbey, quarrying them for stones to use in his new showpiece.

One version of the story of the curse insists that it was this desecration that ultimately called down the wrath of a former Benedictine monk at Battle Abbey. Not only had Sir Anthony Browne, himself a Catholic, shamelessly profited by the Crown's seizure of the Abbey, but then he had remorselessly evicted the monks from their home. And finally, he had added insult to injury by vandalising the holy site to enhance the glory of Cowdray House!

Some say that the infamous curse was uttered by the last monk to leave the premises; others claim that it was delivered by the Abbot of Battle himself. Another version claims that the sub-prioress of Easebourne pronounced it, while another, the most fanciful of all, says that the malediction was proclaimed not by a flesh-and-blood brother, but by a sinister ghostly one who vanished into thin air when guards nearby tried to grab the arms of his cloak. The stories vary also about whether the curse was uttered at the time the monks were evicted or during a banquet given by Sir Anthony in the Abbot's Hall. According to this version, a feast was being held to celebrate Sir Anthony's ownership of the Abbey, and the monk, in either phantom or actual physical form and in a scene reminiscent of Shakespeare's *Macbeth,* appeared as the revellers sat down to eat. (For a full, authoritative account of Cowdray's history and its curse, see Nigel Sadler's website at http://www.nsadler.demon.co.uk/archaeology/cowdray/cowdray.htm.)

Whatever the circumstances of the curse, it has become the most famous and devastatingly effective one in all Sussex history. Sir Anthony Browne was cursed 'in sleeping and waking, in eating and drinking, in his incomings and outgoings'. But of most chilling significance was the pronouncement that his 'line should perish by fire and water'.

The curse was fulfilled, but not until more than two hundred and fifty years had passed. Up to that time, the Browne family continued to prosper. Sir Anthony's son of the same name, also a staunch Roman Catholic, was created the first Viscount Montague by Queen Mary in 1554. By the eighteenth century, Cowdray had evolved into what Horace Walpole called that 'loveliest and perfectest of all ancient mansions'. Not only Walpole, but Samuel Johnson and James Boswell also visited the stately home, widely regarded as one of the most beautiful and charming in England.

Then, in 1793, double disaster struck. The eighth Viscount Montague, George Samuel Browne, was travelling on the Continent while Cowdray House was being redecorated, and his wife and daughter were staying in Brighton (an alternate version suggests that he was still single, and that the manor was being redecorated in honour of his approaching marriage). On 24 September, a careless workman left a piece of charcoal smouldering in an upper room. When it fell onto some wood shavings on the floor, the house was enveloped in a fierce blaze, and soon nothing but ruins were left. Destroyed along with the building and its many art treasures were relics from Battle Abbey, among them the sword and coronation robe of William the Conqueror, as well as the Roll of Battle Abbey, a list of Norman knights read out on the morning that the Battle of Hastings took place, on 14 October 1066.

Most accounts agree that the young heir was spared news of the destruction of his home, but for the most tragic reason. A few days after the fire he drowned during a foolhardy attempt to shoot the rapids of the waterfalls of Lauffen, near Schaffhausen on the Rhine in Germany. Some say that the

Viscount's valet, perhaps remembering the family curse, was said to have tried in vain to restrain his young master by force. Nigel Sadler, however, claims that Browne was actually in the company of a friend, Charles Sedley Burdett, who also drowned. Chroniclers are fond of the story that messengers sent from England to inform the Viscount of the fire crossed paths with other messengers sent from Germany to bring news of the same man's death. Still others say that the Viscount himself received news of the fire immediately before his fateful trip to the waterfalls. But according to Sadler, the letter giving details of the fire arrived too late for Browne to see it. If he had read such a letter, Sadler notes, he may well have abandoned any plans to court further disaster by going near water!

The next heir to Cowdray was the Viscount's cousin, a Franciscan friar, who received from the pope a dispensation to marry and so carry on the line. The man did marry in 1797 but died the same year without leaving a child. The estate then passed on to the Viscount's sister Elizabeth, wife of William Stephen Poyntz. The couple had two sons who were killed in a boating accident in 1815 while the family was on holiday at Bognor. Elizabeth's husband was saved, but her sons drowned while she and the boys' sisters looked on in horror. With this final disaster by water, the Browne line came to an end, in eerie fulfilment of the curse. But some people believe that even though the line was destroyed as prophesied, the evil curse still has power to blight lives. As an example, they point to the 1931 fire that gutted the Abbot's House, the same remodelled by Sir Anthony Browne for his own use.

Other people, refusing to believe that a curse ever existed, say that the legend was made up after the awful events as a way to explain them. But in 1851, a curator at Easebourne was said to have written that he had frequently heard villagers talking about the curse, and that they had believed word of it to have been handed down by servants of the Browne family.

Whether the cursing of the family was an actual historical event or not, after the multiple tragedies, the Cowdray estates were purchased by people who were not related to the Brownes. In the early twentieth century, Sir Weetman Dickinson Pearson, Baronet (the first Viscount Cowdray) conserved the ruins with the help of architect Sir Aston Webb, enabling them to keep standing for another few centuries. It's likely that as long as the ruins exist, so will the spooky legends. For besides that of the curse, there are two other, closely connected tales of the supernatural at Cowdray.

Both stories begin with the fifth Viscount Montague, who had a reputation as a wicked, foul-tempered man. He was forced to go into hiding for fifteen years, until the end of his life, for the murder of a priest. Just as with the tale of the curse, different versions of this story also exist. Some say that the priest was shot dead during a dispute in the confessional, while others say that he was killed for starting Mass before the Viscount arrived! Ironically, considering the identity of

the victim, the Viscount's hiding place was a six-foot-square 'priest-hole' in the keeper's lodge that had been provided by his ancestors centuries earlier.

The Viscount's existence must have been a miserable one, as he left his cramped quarters only in the dead of night to meet his wife, who brought him food and other creature comforts. Probably in the hope that she would be mistaken for a ghost and so deter onlookers, she wore a long white dress that helped to fuel the legend. This sad routine was repeated until the Viscount died in his self-imposed captivity in 1717. His troubled spirit was said to haunt the room until it burned along with most of the rest of the house in 1793.

The second ghost is, of course, the Viscount's wife, said to float down the so-called 'Lady's Walk' on summer evenings. Andrew Green in *Haunted Sussex Today* wonders why it is only the lady's ghost and not that of her husband as well who has been seen on the pathway. Green goes on to relate that in 1994 a young couple saw the phantom during an all-night party. They had wandered away from the rest of the group when they saw the spectral figure walking slowly toward them on the path. As they watched, she suddenly vanished (Seaford, East Sussex: S.B. Publications, 1997, 54-55.)

Although the Cowdray House and Park Ruins are privately owned and at the time of writing not opened for tours as such, those wishing to see them can get an excellent view by walking the short distance along the entrance causeway from Midhurst. Visitors may or may not see any ghosts, but they cannot fail to be moved by the haunting atmosphere evoked by some of the loveliest and most tragic ruins in England.

Firle Place

NEAR LEWES, EAST SUSSEX

When Deborah Gage was growing up, no one was allowed to talk about the ghosts at Firle Place for fear of scaring off the servants. Yet every once in a while, someone would whisper tales to her of the headless horseman, the haunted bedroom, or the weeping woman.

Deborah spent her early years in Africa before returning to England in her teens. She lived near Firle Place and came to visit her relatives there nearly every day. 'None of the stories is very well substantiated,' she told me, 'and one wonders how accurate they are. The subject of ghosts was always very hush hush over the years, but because I was the one involved with the archives, occasionally people would tell me things.'

The father of the present Lord Gage once told her about the headless horseman galloping up the hill through the woods. 'But the wood isn't there any longer - it's been blown down,' Deborah explained. 'I don't know who the ghost was supposed to be or why he was there.'

Before I talked with Deborah, I encountered what might be an interesting connection to this story in a footnote to an unrelated article published in 1939 in *The Sussex County Magazine* (John Playford, 'Alleged Mysterious Happenings at Rye in 1607,' Vol. 13, 808-10, footnote, 810). The editor's note defined the word 'shayishe' from Playford's article, explaining, 'This word is so spelt in the original. Probably it means a faint ray of light; the word, with this meaning, was once used in Kent and Sussex. Once upon a time an "enormous white horse with a bluish shay" (according to a native) was said to haunt Firle Park, near Lewes.'

No rider, headless or otherwise, is mentioned in the footnote, but it is tempting to wonder whether the enormous white horse with its eerie blue light has anything to do with the story Lord Gage told to Deborah.

She was also told about the ghost who walks in and out of the Blue Bedroom, today often referred to as the Queen Mother's Bedroom, as that is where she used to sleep during visits to Firle. The mischievous spirit inhabiting this room likes to play tricks with electricity.

'My father said he slept there one night and woke up to find all the lights blazing,' Deborah remembered. 'So he said to the ghost, "Look, would you mind turning the lights off? I want to go to sleep!" The ghost was very obliging and the lights went off! Nobody knows if this ghost is male or female, and my father may have been embroidering the tale a bit. But I have also heard from others that the room is haunted.'

Perhaps the ghost who usually frequents the Blue Bedroom is the same one who scared the wits out of a young man in the early 1980s. A long-time member of staff at Firle Place recalled the incident for me: 'One night about nine o'clock, we had a film company here. A young electrician was working up in one of the corridors, installing a fitting for the period film they were making. All of a sudden, he came flying down the stairs and out of the door like a bat out of hell!

'We went up to check what had gone wrong and found live wires sticking out of a wall. The guy in charge wanted to sack the electrician for running off the site and leaving bare wires. But when the rest of the film crew finally caught up with him back where they were staying, he was still in a state of absolute terror.

'He said he was working on the light switch when he suddenly felt the hairs on the back of his neck go up. He felt a presence and was very frightened, but when he looked around, there was nobody there. So he just ran.'

Few of the ghost stories at Firle Place are so frightening. Most people who claim to have sensed a presence there, in fact, have felt it to be comforting and friendly. And while details are sketchy, rumours persist about both a Blue Lady and a 'tall woman in grey', with some identifying the latter as Margaret Kemble. She was the American wife of Thomas Gage, General and Commander-in-Chief of the British Army who was disastrously defeated in 1775 at the Battle of Bunker Hill. The daughter of a loyalist family in Morris Town, New Jersey, Margaret Kemble never lived at Firle Place, but she did visit her husband's ancestral home and today lies buried in the churchyard.

Deborah Gage has always been fascinated by Margaret Kemble and plans someday to write a book about her. But she does not believe that Margaret's ghost haunts Firle Place, and she dismisses the stories of the Blue and Grey Ladies. But one Firle ghost story that she does not dismiss is that of the Weeping Lady.

'I find this one to be the most believable,' she told me. 'The mother and aunts of the current Lord Gage all saw her, but I don't think that anyone in the present generation has seen her. The ghost is that of a lady sitting at the foot of the stairs of the Little Hall. She's wearing one of those pointy wimple hats, and people have not only seen her, but they've heard her weeping. At the same time, coming from upstairs are sounds of music, laughter, and gaiety, as if a party is going on.

'I'm not psychic, but I'm sensitive to these things, and sometimes I've felt a presence in the Little Hall, whereas I've never had that experience in the Blue Bedroom or anywhere else. That's why I say that if any of the ghost stories at Firle are believable, it's that of the Weeping Woman.'

Deborah admits, however, that one aspect of the sighting is problematical. Pointed headpieces of the type she describes were popular with upper class women as late as the fifteenth century, but at that time the steps that the lady sits on hadn't been built yet.

'There is another ghost story at Firle, but I don't know how true it is,' Deborah continued. 'The family were Catholics until the eighteenth century, and at one time the house was constantly searched for priests. Years later, two skeletons, believed to be those of priests, were discovered in a secret room downstairs. The skeletons were rushed out of the house to be buried in Firle churchyard so their spirits wouldn't continue to haunt the house. I think that the finding of the skeletons actually happened, but I can't give you any more information.'

Aficionados of both ghosts and fine houses can hardly find a better place to visit than Firle Place, the home of the Gage family for more than five hundred years. In addition to its panoply of spirits, Firle Place also boasts a wealth of paintings, fine furniture, and ceramics, all surrounded by sweeping lawns and beautifully tended gardens.

Just one word of caution, however. As you make the long walk up to the front entrance, do watch out for any headless horsemen galloping by!

Goodwood House

NEAR CHICHESTER, WEST SUSSEX

Goodwood House, home of the Dukes of Richmond since 1697, is also the home of both horse and motor racing in Sussex. But this Jacobean house, built originally as a hunting lodge in about 1616, is apparently home to very few, if any, ghosts.

Rosemary Baird, curator of the Goodwood Collection, told me that she knew of only one tantalising but vague reference to the supernatural there. David Hunn's book, *Goodwood* (1975), quotes a letter from the Duchess of Richmond to her husband in which she was listing rooms for guests. Among other possibilities, such as 'Lord Middlesex's new room', she also mentions 'the haunted room' but gives no details.

'It sounds as if it was in the row of rooms above the Long Hall,' Rosemary explained. 'It could even be a gable room that was subsequently demolished, so I fear we do not know the exact location. The house was only just over one hundred years old at the time.'

We may never know which room it was, who was haunting it, or why. Equally vague was a reference I found on a website regarding a picture taken at what had been a burned out building at Goodwood. A photographer snapping a picture at the renovated building imagined that the photo 'possibly' contained the image of a ghostly monk - or was it just a 'weird shadow'? When I last checked, the web page was no longer there, and the site itself belongs not to any Sussex researchers, but to the West Midlands Ghost Club (see www.cyberpunks.pwp.blueyonder.co.uk).

Another website claims that the nearby woods of Goodwood are the setting for a strange legend about a ghostly calf. In this story, a Viking raiding party stopped at the ancient hillfort, the Trundle, to bury some treasure. The Vikings left a ghostly calf to guard the treasure while they went off to Kingley Vale to fight the men of Chichester. The Vikings were defeated, however, so their treasure remains where it was hidden, and the ghostly calf is said to be heard crying from time to time.

This story has an obvious connection to another legend, that golden calves such as those mentioned in the Old Testament were buried both at Trundle and at another Sussex hillfort, Highdown Hill. The Devil was said to prevent any searchers from digging them up. The Vikings apparently had enough treasure to make their own golden calf, so that is presumably why the guardian of their treasure took the form of that animal. These bits of folklore may have had their origins during the Reformation, when Catholics were believed to bury valuable objects from their churches in order to hide them from reformers (see http://www.homeusers.prestel.co.uk/aspen/sussex/trundle.html).

I was unable to find any more supposedly true ghost stories at Goodwood House, although another kind of unexplained phenomenon - a UFO - was reportedly filmed on a camcorder not once, but two years in a row, by Simon Anderson at the Goodwood Revival Festival. Simon filmed the first incident on 5 September 2003 when a disc-shaped object joined two vintage aircraft that were flying in formation. Amazingly, at the next year's show on 4 September 2004, Simon captured on film a similar metallic-looking disc, flying this time with three World War II fighter planes. Simon's images are clear and easy to make out under perfect blue-sky conditions, and may be viewed at http://www.rense.com/general57/uufo.htm.

Apart from these tales of strange events is a ghost story that is surely fiction. "The Goodwood Ghost Story" appeared anonymously in December 1862 in Charles Dickens's own weekly periodical, *All the Year Round*, and was later published in a collection called *The Haunters and the Haunted*, edited by Ernest Rhys, in 1921. In this collection the story was 'doubtfully attributed to Charles Dickens', but was presented as a true account. Its authorship was revealed later, this time apparently without any doubt, when it appeared in two books edited by Peter Haining, first in *The Complete Ghost Stories of Charles Dickens* in 1983 (London: Franklin Watts) and again in *Charles Dickens' Christmas Ghost Stories* in 1992 (New York: St. Martin's Press).

"The Goodwood Ghost Story" uses Goodwood House not as the setting for the haunting but for some of the central plot elements. The tale involves a widow who is seriously injured in a carriage accident while attending a picnic on the grounds of Goodwood House. She is taken to a nearby inn, where she returns to consciousness only briefly and attempts to speak, but cannot. At that moment, while she is still alive, her ghost is seen in her sister's stable, miles away, but the sister believes that she is seeing a flesh-and-blood creature. Hours later, the widow dies, leaving her two young daughters homeless and penniless. For two years they are cared for in turn by various relatives. At the end of the story, the narrator encounters the widow's ghost on a snowy road late at night. Without saying a word, the apparition makes him understand that she wants him to take care of her girls. The narrator gives his promise, wipes the cold perspiration from his face, and when he looks up again, the spirit has disappeared.

Just like the phantom in Dickens's story, the ghosts of Goodwood House and the surrounding areas, if they ever existed, may have vanished. But if you go to any of the air shows at Goodwood, who knows? You might just be lucky enough to see a UFO!

The Grange
ROTTINGDEAN, EAST SUSSEX

Known as the vicarage of St Margaret's Church for two hundred and fifty years, this fine early Georgian house beside the village pond was renamed 'The Grange' by artist Sir William Nicholson, who lived here in the years immediately prior to the First World War. Built around 1740 on the site of a much earlier building, the residence was home in the late eighteenth century to Dr Thomas Hooker, vicar of Rottingdean. His school on the premises educated several boys who would go on to become famous, including Cardinal Henry Manning and the novelist Edward Bulwer-Lytton. Enlarged by architect Sir Edwin Lutyens in the 1920s, The Grange now serves as a museum, art gallery and library administered by the Rottingdean Preservation Society. Several exhibits are devoted to former residents of the area, including Rudyard Kipling, who knew it from childhood days spent with an aunt and uncle, and who later lived in a house called 'The Elms' situated just across the green.

But the legendary ghost haunting The Grange has nothing to do with these ecclesiastical or literary figures. According to John Rackham's *Brighton Ghosts, Hove Hauntings,* the phantom is the Black Prince, eldest son of Edward III, who in 1355 is believed to have stayed at the original house constructed on the site. For some unknown reason, on dark and stormy nights the Black Prince occasionally returns for a repeat visit and has been seen 'clambering across the roof' ('Smugglers and spectres,'Brighton: Latimer Publications, 2001, 235-36).

Rackham attributes tales of the spectral Black Prince to someone's overactive imagination, but he admits that the experience of a waitress in the spring of 1996 is harder to explain away. One day while working at the tearoom in The Grange, she headed for the storeroom at the rear. As she unlocked the door, she felt the air around her suddenly grow cold, and at the same time, she became aware of an unearthly presence nearby. She was so upset that she quit her job, and a priest in charge of St Margaret's Church was called in to perform a kind of exorcism.

The priest's prayers must have worked, because according to Grange coordinator Brian Wholey, the property today has a very friendly, welcoming atmosphere. Brian told me that he had never heard any ghost stories associated with The Grange, in fact, and that although he has spent much time there alone, he has never been frightened in the least. It would appear that the only kind of 'spirit' visitors are likely to encounter nowadays is the spirit of Rottingdean's past, which continues to be charmingly preserved at The Grange.

Groombridge Place Gardens

Near Tunbridge Wells, in East Sussex

Sir Arthur Conan Doyle, creator of the famous detective Sherlock Holmes, knew and loved Groombridge Place. For over thirty years he lived in Crowborough, four miles away, and was a frequent visitor to the seventeenth-century moated manor house near the Kent border. One of his favourite pastimes was participating in the séances held there by his friends, Louisa and Eliza Saint. So taken was Conan Doyle by the property that he used it as the setting for his 1915 mystery *The Valley of Fear,* changing its name to 'Birlstone Manor'.

Given Conan Doyle's predilection for the paranormal and his obvious attachment to Groombridge Place, it is perhaps surprising that it is not his ghost who wanders the grounds today. That honour belongs instead to a nineteenth-century ostler named Dave Fletcher, but it was Sir Arthur Conan Doyle who brought this unfortunate phantom to the attention of the world.

In *At the Edge of the Unknown,* a non-fiction work exploring occult themes, Conan Doyle describes his own meeting with the ghost. One afternoon he was visiting Groombridge Place in the company of American friends, Dr and Mrs Wickland. Dr Wickland was a serious student of psychic phenomena, and his wife was a renowned medium. They were examining the lichened brick walls, Conan Doyle writes, when 'a door which gave upon the deep moat opened and a woman looked out. Then it closed again. We passed on, and I thought no more of the matter.'

As the trio walked through the meadow leading to the road, Mrs Wickland kept glancing over her shoulder, claiming that they were being followed by an earth-bound spirit, an old man with a sunken face and a hunched back. The party made their way to the Crown Inn in the village, where they had tea. Mrs Wickland kept glancing at a chair in the corner beside her, claiming that the spirit was still with them. Later, when they were all seated among the roses on Conan Doyle's veranda, Mrs Wickland suddenly went into an unexpected trance, her face transforming itself before them as the spirit of an old man finally took possession of her.

Through the session that followed, it was established that the spirit's name was Dave Fletcher, and that he had been an ostler at Groombridge Place. He had lived with his mother in the cottage beside the moat, where he had drowned in 1808. He was ashamed of the hump on his back, and because he 'looked queer', no one had loved him after his mother died. He had had a good master in the house, but when the old master died, Dave had not liked the 'others' who came in. The house was sold, and the servants weren't treated well after that. Someone named Sam had pushed him into the moat, but Dave didn't realise he was dead until Dr Wickland convinced him it was true.

Dr Wickland continued to speak soothingly to the spirit until he was able at last to escape to the higher realms. 'And so it was,' Conan Doyle explains, 'that the earth-bound ostler found his mother at last among the rambler roses of my balcony.'

Barbara Maidment in *A History of Groombridge Place* says that subsequent sightings of Dave Fletcher's ghost have been reported at the manor, so perhaps the Wicklands weren't able to free him after all. Or perhaps he just likes to return from time to time to a place where he once knew a small measure of earthly happiness. Visitors likewise can wander the grounds, although the house is not open to the public.

Hammerwood Park

NEAR EAST GRINSTEAD, WEST SUSSEX

Even without its reputation for having a ghost or two, Hammerwood Park would be one of the most interesting and unusual stately homes to visit in Sussex. When John Sperling had the mansion built in 1792, he chose for its architect Benjamin Henry Latrobe, who would later go on to America to design both the White House and the Capitol in Washington, D.C. Hammerwood Park was Latrobe's first architectural work, and it was likewise one of the first buildings in England to be constructed in the Greek Revival style. Originally conceived as a temple to Apollo, the god of both arts and the hunt, Hammerwood was intended for use, appropriately enough, as a hunting lodge.

The graceful mansion also served as home to a series of families until the Second World War, when it was requisitioned by the military to become the quarters for some two hundred soldiers. Afterwards, the house was divided into eleven flats in an attempt to ensure its long-term preservation. By this time, however, dry rot had begun to set in, and the flats were eventually vacated. The musical group Led Zeppelin bought Hammerwood Park in 1973, intending to turn it into a recording studio and housing for their families, but because of increasing commitments abroad and worsening dry rot, this plan was never realised. Left vacant too long, the house was also vandalised during this period. Three tons of lead was stripped from the roof, allowing massive amounts of water to enter and to cause even more destruction.

In 1976, Latrobe's once-grand showpiece was boarded up and offered for sale, but its dilapidated condition discouraged buyers. Finally, in 1982, the house found its saviour in twenty-one-year-old David Pinnegar. David, who came from a family of conservationists, had inherited his grandmother's house. When he sold that, he was able to buy Hammerwood Park and to set about the long process of restoring it. Individual craftsmen and volunteers have performed much of the work, and their efforts have been rewarded with several international awards. English Heritage has provided some funding, without which the repairs could not have been accomplished. Much more restoration is still to be done, and David remains committed to the task. Now living at Hammerwood Park with his wife and family, he also runs the house as a bed and breakfast establishment, opening it as well for concerts, charity events, and tours.

Even though the Pinnegars haven't seen or heard any ghosts themselves, they keep open minds on the subject. David told me of one story involving an American soldier who stayed in the house during the Second World War. 'He apparently shot himself on the stairs in the main hall, whether by accident or not we don't know,' David said. 'He is meant to haunt the hall.

'We've also had psychics here who claim to have picked up all sorts of vibrations, telling us, for example, about the ghost of a former housekeeper who complained about the fact that we now have electricity. After all, as she told them, 'It is so much more difficult to dim the electric bulbs than to flicker a candle!'

David takes the claims of psychics with 'half a pinch of salt', but he admits that, occasionally, they do manage to turn up information that would be very difficult or even impossible to acquire by more traditional means. 'I'm a sceptic, but I've been shocked enough to sit up and take notice because of some of the things they said,' he explained.

A case in point is the visit of four psychics who came to Hammerwood Park in November 1996 for a fundraising 'Spookathon' for charity. 'I don't want to be too specific,' David said, 'but they picked up information about one of the nineteenth-century owners of the house and his son that was in line with what we knew from talking to one of the descendants of the family. The psychics could not have got that information from those people.'

This incident, described on the Hammerwood Park website, involved the ghosts arguing as to whether they wanted to be referred to as a 'marchant' or a 'merchant' family (http://www.mistral.co.uk/hammerwood/ghosts.htm). Upon being informed of the spirits' spat, we are told, a descendant of the family confirmed that there had indeed been talk of the father being 'rather aware of his merchant background and wanting his son to be more of a gentleman'.

David told me about another incident in which psychics picked up vibrations of a maidservant who drowned in a lake. 'Reputedly, she died because the son of the family was "too keen" on her, if you know what I mean,' David said. 'It's interesting that the family who were here in the 1930s also talked about the ghost of a lonely housemaid. She was said to haunt bachelors who stayed in the west wing. When you find stories that tie together as well as that, you start wondering whether the psychics might have a point.'

'In connection with the story about the housemaid, I know that Hammerwood was let out to a family in the latter stages of the First World War,' David continued, 'and there are anecdotal stories about the tenants. I don't know who they were, but apparently one day an incident occurred that resulted in police being called to the house. Locals in the area were aware of this story, and one just wonders whether it involved the housemaid.'

'Psychics have also said that there were children here who died of some disease,' David said. 'Other people have sensed that as well, but I've had no evidence of it. The house may have its ghosts, but they keep themselves to themselves, and our guests have reported nothing. The psychics tell us that our ghosts are perfectly happy, which is why they don't draw attention to themselves too much!'

Apparently, no ghost is happier at Hammerwood Park than that of its architect, Benjamin Henry Latrobe. On their 1996 visit to the house, the four psychics claimed to channel an early New Year's message from the great man, full of gratitude and encouragement to the Pinnegars for their ongoing restoration efforts. 'I assist where and when I can to help David meet his aims,' the spirit is supposed to have said, adding that although the house was not his most famous work, it was his 'favourite of all time'. The spirit of Latrobe then promised to help the Pinnegars recapture the finery of the house, assuring them that the project would take 'many years to complete' but that it would be a wonderful achievement with which they would not be disappointed.

Latrobe's spirit may not be quite so contented with one of his more famous creations. Jim Abrams, an Associated Press writer, on 30 October 2003 published a tale about the haunted Capitol in Washington, D.C. The story appeared in many US newspapers, describing demon cats that walk the halls along with spectres of assassinated presidents, and statues that descend from their pedestals to dance midnight minuets. Abrams reports that the Capitol got off to a bad start in 1808 when construction superintendent John Lenthall argued with Latrobe over the vaulting in what is now known as the Old Supreme Court Chamber. When Lenthall tried to remove braces from the vaulting, the ceiling collapsed, crushing him. With his dying breath, the legend says, Lenthall put a curse on the Capitol.

Fortunately, for visitors and family members alike, no such curse has befallen Latrobe's charming first creation back in Sussex. If anything, the reverse seems to be true. Hammerwood Park, now well on the way to resuming its former glory, appears to have been decidedly blessed.

Hastings Castle
HASTINGS, EAST SUSSEX

ho, looking at the ancient, crumbling ruins of Hastings Castle today, would ever believe that this was, in fact, England's first prefab building? Whereas most people probably associate such construction techniques with the modern era, way back in 1066, when William the Conqueror crossed the Channel, he brought along several prefabricated timber forts. One was taken to Hastings and erected on the West Hill, becoming not only the first prefab structure to be built in the country, but also the first castle in England to be constructed wholly by Normans. Shortly thereafter, when Robert, Count of Eu, was granted the Rape of Hastings, he replaced the wooden building with a more durable one of stone, incorporating the Collegiate Church of St Mary within its walls.

Although Hastings Castle never saw much fighting, it is believed to have been the scene of the first tournament in England, held for Adela, William's daughter. The castle also served an important function when Hastings was the port of embarkation for Normandy, until 1204, when King John lost his French possessions. Twelve years later he had the castle temporarily dismantled, as he feared a French invasion that might use coastal fortifications as bases. In 1287 storms swept away a large part of the cliff on which the castle was built. The keep was destroyed and the harbour silted up, ending the town's usefulness as a port. The castle thus lost its military significance, although it continued to be a religious house until the Dissolution of the Monasteries. The Pelham family took possession of the castle from 1591 to 1951, when the Hastings Corporation finally purchased it.

Neglect, erosion, and natural disasters have destroyed much of the once proud fortification, but ghostly echoes of the past remain. Some say, in fact, that Hastings Castle itself has become a ghost. According to this legend, when the sun is bright but mist covers the sea, a life-sized manifestation of the structure may appear floating on the horizon. Fishermen and sailors several miles from shore are said to have seen this spectacular vision. Such sightings could normally be explained as a mirage, except that the castle appears not as the ruin it is now, but whole and new as it was in the eleventh century, complete with flags and banners billowing out from walls and turrets.

As far as I know, no one has reported seeing this splendid apparition for some time, if indeed it was ever seen at all. But other stories of the supernatural may not be dismissed so easily. Take, for example, the legend of ghostly music said to emanate from the ruins of the castle church. The swell of organ music and the sounds of chanting are heard periodically, and in November 2000 a large crowd, congregated on the seafront for a fireworks display, was said to have been startled by the unexplained fanfare of trumpets echoing from the castle walls (http://www.ghosts-uk.net/modules/news/article.php?storyid=273).

Less melodious are the sounds of groans and rattling chains that reportedly arise from the dungeons. These underground chambers were carved from the part of the structure known as the Mount, and they may still be found in the ruins of the old gatehouse. The noises are believed to be the phantom echoes of starving prisoners, moaning in agony and begging for food.

A ghostly drummer boy is also supposed to haunt Hastings Castle, but I was unable to find any details about him. It seems likely, as many writers suggest, that this phantom was invented by smugglers to keep the curious away from their illegal activities. But what about the tales of the spectre of Thomas Becket, who was once Dean of the church college here? The ghost of the murdered Archbishop of Canterbury has been reported within the precincts of the castle grounds. For some reason, he appears only on autumn evenings, strolling about the ruins and occasionally gazing out to sea.

The most commonly sighted phantoms at Hastings Castle are those of women, however. It seems likely that there are at least two of them, although witnesses are often unsure about which one they have seen. The confusion probably arises because both ghosts are usually said to wear brown - one is clad in the habit of a medieval nun, or a brown cloak, while the other is adorned in a dress of the Victorian era.

These figures have been seen both at the western and eastern ends of the castle, and at least two photographs have been taken that purport to show a female apparition. According to one website, witnesses have seen a phantom nun who digs 'ferociously with her hands near the entrance to where the dungeons and prisons once stood'. The writer wonders whether the nun is trying vainly to escape after being held prisoner at the castle because of her religious beliefs (http://perso.libertysurf.co.uk/markwd56/southeast_castles1e.htm).

Tony Wales in *Sussex Ghosts & Legends* writes that the popular idea is that the 'nun in a brown habit, who has been seen digging' was put to death for breaking her vows. He adds that a caretaker and his wife are supposed to have seen her quite regularly, and that a visitor once captured her image on film. Wales also claims that a medium from London went into a trance and made contact with the nun, but he includes no further details (Newbury, Berkshire: Countryside Books, 1992, 51).

Andrew Green in his *Ghosts of Today* also writes of the 'nun in brown, seen digging a few feet from the entrance to a dungeon'. He points out that this phantom cannot be dismissed merely as a smugglers' invention, as she has been seen several times since the Victorian period. He surmises that she might be a sister hiding some of the church plate from the Cromwellians, adding that a figure believed to be the same woman has also been seen near the outer wall at the eastern end of Hastings Castle. Green goes on to claim that a woman in a nun's habit was photographed in the summer of 1976, appearing in the developed photo as a third figure alongside two friends who were visiting the site. The figure was not visible when the picture was taken (London: Kaye & Ward, 1980, 37-38).

In *Haunted Sussex Today,* Green writes again of the 'phantom nun, or a woman wearing a brown cloak or hood' who appears on the West Hill below the castle. He adds that in 1976 the widow of a former custodian claimed to have seen the ghost and to have identified her as Agnes Silby, lover of a fourteenth-century dean of the king's free chapel located inside the castle walls. Green mentions also that a visitor's photograph taken in 1979 showed the 'vague figure' of a woman bending down as if she were looking for something within a few feet of a wall. He speculates that she might have been searching for buried treasure or even digging a grave (Seaford, East Sussex: S.B. Publications, 1997, 37-38).

In both books, Green admits that the apparitions of the nun and the Victorian woman may sometimes have been mistaken for each other, presumably because they have often manifested so indistinctly. But in *Ghosts of Today* he writes that the spectre of the Victorian woman in a brown dress has been seen more frequently than that of the nun. She seems to be carrying a baby in her arms and hesitates for a few moments before moving decisively toward the cliff, at which point both she and the child vanish. This ghost, Green says, is believed to be a local woman who was abandoned by her fisherman lover after giving birth to his illegitimate daughter. In despair, she disposed of both her baby and herself by jumping from the cliff. Another writer, Tony Ellis, adds that the incident involving the 'young girl' and her infant occurred in 1840, and that there were several others who similarly plunged to their deaths in the eighteenth and nineteenth centuries (from *Ghosts of the South East, Part Two* by Tony Ellis, http://members.aol.com/MercStG2/GOSEENGPage2.html).

Might one of those suicides account for the phantom seen by Betty Palmer when she was a child in the early 1930s? Betty, who grew up close to the castle in a house on top of the West Hill, has never forgotten the apparition she saw when she was about five and a half years old.

'It must have been a Monday,' Betty told me, 'and as my mother was changing the bed linen, I'd sat myself down in the garden to amuse myself. We had a very ancient and huge black Persian cat, and it was sitting asleep in the sun, on top of the high garden gate. I was throwing my ball up to the gate and catching it as it came back.

'Suddenly, the cat screeched and arched its back! With all its fur standing on end, it shot right across to the left. Now, this cat normally never ran for any reason, and took ages even to come after its food, but here it was acting like a spring chicken! I'd never seen it do anything like that, and I turned around to see what was happening.'

'Through the gate came this woman, walking without making a sound, floating down the path toward me,' Betty recalled. 'She just came clean through the gate, and the gate remained shut. She was sort of half-smiling and wearing a long white or pearl-grey dress, a simple garment from an earlier time. She was a young, sweet-looking thing. I wasn't frightened, only surprised to see someone in the garden who shouldn't have been there.'

'I shouted, "Mummy!" and rushed indoors. I can still see Mother now. She was tussling to get the pillow in the pillowcase. I said, "There's a strange woman in the garden." Mother looked out and saw nothing at all, and told me that I must have imagined it, and to stop being silly.'

'I knew instinctively that what I had seen was a ghost, even though I was quite an isolated child and had no means of knowing much at all about such things,' Betty insisted. 'The only person who believed me was my grandmother, who said, "If Betty said she saw it, she saw it."

'That ended the conversation and it was never mentioned again for years. But when my mother was in her seventies, I brought up the time I'd seen a ghost, and she said, "Good Lord, do you still remember that?" And I said, "Yes, like yesterday."'

'Information has come forth to suggest that this ghost does indeed haunt the area,' Betty continued. 'About twenty or thirty years ago, I saw on television that a party of guides at the castle claimed that several children, sensible girls, had said that they saw a lady walk right across the fire of a barbecue they were having. Of course, the guide captain thought that the children were pulling their legs, but when they researched the story, they found that over the years, a ghostly woman had been seen only by children, never adults. She is said to appear and to walk through solid objects.'

'Because she only appears to children, I wonder if she's the one I saw,' Betty said. 'Because our house was only spitting distance from the castle.'

Yet another female ghost is rumoured to haunt St Mary-in-the-Castle, a church built into the cliff rocks immediately below the old Norman fortification. This building on the seafront, constructed during the Georgian era and now used as an arts centre, is haunted by the spectre of a young girl buried in the crypt. Victoria Seymour, a writer on Sussex history during the Second World War, told me that the girl is believed to have died of typhus, and that many staff members have seen her. Victoria interviewed one tour guide who claimed not to believe in ghosts but who nevertheless had a very unsettling experience. One winter evening after closing the building, the guide noticed a young woman sitting in the balcony pews. She had long dark hair hanging over her shoulders and was wearing a shawl. 'Thinking that I had locked in a visitor, I went to speak to her,' the guide said, 'but she just melted away.'

That's the trouble with ghosts - they tend just to melt away, often before astonished witnesses have had the chance to take in the full import of what they've observed. But ghosts often make reappearances, too - sometimes even in photographs, as they've done repeatedly at Hastings Castle. Visitors to the first Norman fortification in England may not experience anything out of the ordinary while they're there, but who knows what they might find when they take a look at their pictures afterwards?

Hastings Museum
& Art Gallery, Hastings, East Sussex

The beautiful building now housing the Hastings Museum & Art Gallery, constructed in the second half of the nineteenth century, was once the home of Mrs Frances Kidd. In 1914, Mrs Kidd's son John, like so many others of his generation, was caught up in the tragedy of the First World War. He interrupted his medical studies to join the army, and in 1916 he was killed in the Battle of the Somme.

Heartbroken, Mrs Kidd found it too painful to continue living in a house that contained so many memories of her son. A few years after his death, she decided to sell it to the Council at a reduced rate.

In 1912 the Hastings Museum moved into the building, where it has continued to enrich the cultural life of the area ever since. Since then, about half a dozen visitors have claimed that they could sense an invisible presence in the museum, particularly in the Upper Durbar Hall, an extension added on to the building in 1931.

The elaborate woodcarvings and furnishings of the Durbar Hall were created originally for the Colonial and Indian Exhibition held in South Kensington in 1886. Intended to represent a typical Indian royal residence, Durbar Hall was one of the most popular features of the Exhibition, and its upper storey was used for official receptions of the Prince of Wales.

After the Exhibition, Durbar Hall was acquired by the first Lord Brassey as a museum extension to his home at 24 Park Lane in London. There it displayed the ethnographic collection of Lady Brassey, as well as other works of art from the Exhibition, acquired in turn from various parts of India and Tibet. From 1889-1918 the Lady Brassey Museum in the Durbar Hall was open by arrangement to interested parties, and in 1919 the second Lord Brassey presented the building and many of the works of art to the town of Hastings, where it was built on as an extension to Mrs Kidd's former house in 1931.

No one can say for sure just who the ghost might be, but it is best known for its mischievous nature. A part-time staff member working as a cleaner was startled to find that her Hoover had switched off at the wall plug while she was using it in Durbar Hall. Another staff member attributes most of the visitor tales of a strange presence in the building to its preponderance of woodcarvings and exotic artefacts.

'Perhaps they create a spooky feeling for some people,' he said, 'but I find this to be a calming and magical place.'

Heaven Farm

NEAR UCKFIELD, EAST SUSSEX

istoric Heaven Farm, with its nature trail, wallabies, and Sussex Rural Life Museum is the perfect place to spend a relaxing day in the countryside. Constructed in the 1820s, the buildings on site today contain re-used timbers from the previous farm which dated from the fourteenth century. Adding to the charm of the setting is the fact that the present buildings are almost exactly the same as when they were reconstructed in the nineteenth century.

Current owner John Butler, who has been at Heaven Farm since 1959, attributes the lack of change to the fact that over the past century the property has had only one owner besides himself. And this previous owner seems to be responsible for the ghostly occurrences around the place.

'My predecessor was a recluse here,' John explained, 'the last person of her family. In 1932, when all her other family members had died, she just shut up the bedrooms in the house and continued to live here alone. Eventually, in 1959, she realized that she was dying of cancer, but she wished to live out her life here. The doctor told her that there was no way she could carry on at the farm without some help, so he called on the local land agent, who came to take stock of the situation. On his way back, he passed my father's farm next door and asked if one of us Butler boys would be able to help. My dad agreed, so I came round to see our neighbour through the last months and weeks of her cancer.'

During her final illness, the woman worried about what would happen to all of her animals after she died. 'She came to me one day,' John continued, 'and said, "Oh, Mr Butler, it's such a cruel world! I cannot allow all my animals to leave the farm. I'm going to have them all put down here."'

'She knew that some farmers can be cruel, and she didn't want her animals to be mistreated. I tried to talk her out of it, but she was very determined. That was some terrible experience, I tell you. All the animals were shot except for some half wild cats that escaped. And a man who used to help around here told his wife about what was happening, and she said, "No way are they putting that dog down!" So she came and took the dog and it lived another ten years.'

John Butler continued living at Heaven Farm after his neighbour's death, and as his own family grew up there, it became a much happier place. But even so, some might say that his predecessor has never really left her old home.

'My eldest daughter's former partner witnessed a ghost walking along the landing one day,' John told me. 'He described the person he saw, and she was exactly like the person we had known. But there is no way he could have known what she looked like.'

Another sighting in about 1988 involved John's granddaughter, who was then about four years old. 'She went up to the bedroom and when she came back down she asked, "Mummy, who's that lady I've just seen upstairs in the bedroom?" There was nobody there, of course.'

Heaven Farm was opened to the public in 1986, and while there is no guarantee that visitors will themselves witness anything of the *super*natural there, they will almost certainly find enough pleasures from the *natural* world to make for a wonderful day out.

Herstmonceux Castle

HAILSHAM, EAST SUSSEX

In spite of its name, Herstmonceux Castle has always served as a residence rather than a military stronghold. Since 1441, when Sir Roger Fiennes applied to the king for a licence to 'with walls and lime, enclose, krenellate, entower and embattle his manor of HURST MONCEUX in the County of Sussex', this fortified manor house has never once been besieged. Constructed most likely on the site of the old manor house, the new castle was made of red brick, an unusual material for the time, and is today the oldest brick building of any significance still standing in England. Over the centuries, Herstmonceux Castle has been put to a variety of uses and has played host to some of the county's (if not the country's) most prominent, eccentric, and fascinating people, acquiring more than a few ghosts in the process.

The Domesday Book provides the earliest written record of the manor, then part of the property granted by William the Conqueror to the Count of Eu. By the twelfth century, it had passed to the de Herste family, and when Idonea de Herste married Ingelram de Monceux, the union led to the manor being called the 'Herste of the Monceux' and finally, 'Herstmonceux'. The last male de Monceux to hold the property died in 1330, passing it on to his sister Maud, the wife of Sir John Fiennes.

The Fiennes family were connected by marriage to the Dacres, and one of the most famous ghost stories, that of the Phantom Drummer of Herstmonceux, is thought to involve either the Fiennes or the Dacres. Some claim that the drummer was a servant of the Fiennes family, a soldier who died in 1415 at Agincourt, fighting alongside his master. Unfortunately, this story cannot be verified, for although James Fiennes served with King Henry V in France, there is no proof that he fought in the historic battle. Nevertheless, the ghostly figure is said to march along the castle's southern battlements, beating out a tattoo as he guards a treasure concealed in the recess of a wall. Depending on which version of the tale you prefer, he measures from six to nine feet tall and marches either with or without his head. In some stories, he marches alone, whereas in others he accompanies the castle's private army. Some say that he emits an eerie glow and that sparks fly from his drumsticks.

If the Phantom Drummer is not a former servant of the Fiennes family, he might be the ghost of an eccentric member of the Dacre family. In all versions of this legend that I have found, he is referred to simply as 'Lord Dacre' with no other identifying information, although Peter Underwood suggests that he lived in the nineteenth century (*The A-Z of British Ghosts*, London: Chancellor Press, 1992, 94-95). Marc Alexander writes in *Haunted Castles* that this Lord Dacre was a religious recluse motivated by a desire to retire from the world. In a manner reminiscent of the early Christian anchorites, he shut himself inside a small cell where he lived on a diet of bread and water (London: Frederick Muller, 1974, 86).

To further secure his isolation, the eccentric hermit ordered his beautiful young wife to tell the world that he was dead. Then, to frighten potential suitors away from her, he donned a drummer's uniform and applied phosphorous to his face, his clothing, and his drum before parading the grounds as a ghastly, glowing ghost. When his resentful wife grew tired of this bizarre treatment, she locked him in his cell and withdrew even his bread and water. Lord Dacre then starved to death, but even afterwards, we are told, his ghost, clad in its glowing raiment, kept on drumming and marching around the castle.

Regardless of who the Phantom Drummer is supposed to be, smugglers doubtlessly had their own reasons for spreading tales about him. R. Moore in *Sussex Ghosts* claims that a group of smugglers made the castle their headquarters at a time when it was in ruins, and that they smeared one of their own with phosphorous before sending him out to scare away locals (St Ives, Cornwall: James Pike Ltd, 1976, 12).

Horace Walpole shows another way smugglers exploited the legend in a letter written in 1752. During a visit to the castle, he writes, he was shown 'a dismal chamber which they called the Drummers Hall' that 'took its name from intrigues of Tartare or Tart, a French gardener who alarmed the family by beating after the manner of a drum to frighten the inmates, no doubt to conceal the operations of the smugglers who frequented the Hall and whose friend the gardener was' (reprinted by Andrew Green, *Haunted Sussex Today*, Seaford, East Sussex: S.B. Publications, 1997, 45).

If what the letter says is true, the 'drum' used by the gardener might actually have been an iron chest discovered a few years before Walpole's visit. Judy Middleton in *Ghosts of Sussex* writes that John Miller, a servant of the Hare family, and Will Lancaster, a son of the Steward, chanced upon the chest in the castle's attic one day in 1738. The boys turned a key in the lock and found papers inside, but what excited them most were the two hammer-like, metal objects attached to the chest. The boys removed them and beat them against the chest, creating a sound noticeably like that made by a kettledrum. Thrilled to have found the Drummer's actual instrument, off they went to tell someone, but when they returned, the chest had vanished. In 1892, Middleton goes on to say, the rust-covered chest was found again in the underground passages of the castle and placed in the Guardroom directly below the Drummer's Hall. No one today, however, seems to know where the chest might be (Newbury, Berkshire: Countryside Books, 1988, reprinted 1996, 30-31).

While Sussex smugglers clearly found the story of the Phantom Drummer convenient, either for warding off the curious or for signalling to each other that the coast was clear, it does not appear that they invented the legend as some have suggested, for a clearly labelled 'Drummer's Room', located over the south gateway, appears on a plan of the castle dating from the early eighteenth century, before any smuggling occurred in the vicinity. Besides that, tales of the haunting have persisted up to recent times, long past the heyday of smuggling.

Andrew Green, for example, writes of an incident reported by the Canadian newspaper, the *Victoria Times Colonist*, on 7 December 1994. A film crew with CBC Newsworld had been visiting and were trying to shoot a discussion programme organised for the new owners of Herstmonceux Castle, the Queens University of Kingston, Ontario. As soon as moderator and presenter Alison Smith began speaking, an unidentified 'high keening drumming noise' disrupted the filming. As a result, several hours were lost from the filming schedule, and the mysterious sound ceased only after the film crew admitted to a belief that the castle was haunted. A cameraman, Pascal Leblond, agreed that 'the cause of the trouble was the fun loving ghost of Herstmonceux' (*Haunted Sussex Today*, 45).

Less than two years later, in April 1996, Andrew Green himself held an overnight vigil in the Drummer's Room for two editorial members of *Walt Disney Adventures*. The visitors experienced nothing unusual themselves, but were 'peeved', Green writes, to find out the next morning that at the same time they had been quietly ensconced in the 'haunted' room, staff member Andrea Edwards had heard the mysterious drumming while working on the ground floor just beneath them.

Another ghost with historical ties to Herstmonceux Castle is that of Sir Thomas Fiennes, the third Lord Dacre, sometimes seen riding his magnificent horse in the grounds. Thomas's sad story began on a spring evening in 1541, when he was twenty-five years old. In the company of several friends, he apparently decided to go poaching on the land of Sir Nicholas Pelham of Laughton. When the poachers reached Pikehaie in the parish of Hellingly, they encountered three of Pelham's servants. What happened next and who was to blame has been the subject of much conjecture, but the tragic result was the fatal wounding and death, two days later, of gamekeeper John Busbridge. Thomas and three of his friends were arrested, convicted, and hanged.

The circumstances of Lord Dacre's trial have also provoked much speculation, with his immediate descendants claiming that his only crime was poaching, and that it was never proven that he had even been present at the wounding of the gamekeeper. Therefore, they argued, Thomas may have pleaded guilty only because he anticipated leniency from the crown, perhaps more for his friends than for himself. Some even claimed that Thomas was misled into pleading guilty by false friends who secretly sought his execution in the hope of profiting from the forfeiture of his estates. If such deception occurred, however, it was ineffective, since the legal will of Sir Thomas's grandfather had made sure that the Dacre properties would stay strictly within the family.

Thomas's hanging was unusual for a nobleman, as persons of such rank were generally executed more quickly and humanely by axe. Marc Alexander in *Haunted Castles* claims that the Phantom Drummer was said to have beat an eerie tattoo right before the deaths of Lord Dacre and his friends, all of whose spirits are said to roam the estate on horseback, usually around midnight. The spectre of Lord Dacre has been seen wearing a rust-coloured riding cloak and large brass spurs, and his horse has been variously described as black, brown, or chestnut. Whenever witnesses speak to this phantom, however, he turns away to plunge himself and his horse into the moat.

A later Lord Dacre, Sir Thomas Lennard, fell into financial troubles and was forced to sell Herstmonceux Castle in 1708. Thus the estate passed into the hands of London solicitor George Naylor, whose daughter Grace was to become another well-known phantom of Herstmonceux Castle. According to this oft-told tale, Grace was imprisoned in one of the towers by her governess, who was either bribed by a family member or motivated by her own intense jealousy of the girl (although why she was jealous is never explained). Most versions of the legend say that the governess starved her young charge, who died on the eve of her twenty-first birthday and was thus prevented from coming into her inheritance. A room known as The Lady's Bower is still supposed to resound with the screams and cries of the starving girl, whose emaciated wraith is also seen strolling along the east-wing corridors and as far away as the moat.

Grace's ghost may indeed still walk the halls and grounds of Herstmonceux Castle, but if so, that is the only truthful part of the tale. The fact is that when Grace died in 1727, no one seemed to consider the circumstances of her death suspicious. Judy Middleton in *Ghosts of Sussex* admits that the young heiress is generally agreed to have died of starvation, but claims that her death was probably the result of anorexia nervosa, a condition little understood at the time (Newbury, Berkshire: Countryside Books, 1988, 32).

Grace's father outlived his daughter by only three years, and when he died the estate first went to a nephew and later became the residence of Dr Francis Hare and his wife Bethia, who lived in the castle during the 1730s and 40s. According to David Calvert and Roger Martin, co-authors of *A History of Herstmonceux Castle*, Bethia seems to have suffered from mental illness, and it may have been the strange behaviour of this living woman, rather than the antics of the ghostly Grace, that led to tales of a Grey Lady haunting the property. To add to the confusion, the castle also boasts of visitations by a so-called White Lady, whose own identity is not certain either, and who is herself sometimes described as the Grey Lady!

Many people believe that the White Lady is the ghost of a young woman who was murdered several centuries ago by one of the Fiennes family. Peter Underwood in *The A-Z of British Ghosts* writes that one of the young sons had enticed a village girl into the castle and into his bed. At this point she resisted his advances, however, and fled outside, where she tried to escape by swimming the moat. The man dragged her back into the castle, where he raped and murdered her in what became known as 'the haunted bed', an artefact that Underwood claims was preserved until a few years before his writing. Underwood goes on to claim that local people have seen the ghost of the murdered girl swimming soundlessly in the moat. Others say that the White Lady usually makes her appearance at night, either in the moat itself or standing beside the water wringing her hands.

In the early twentieth century Colonel Claude Lowther, who bought Herstmonceux Castle in 1911, encountered what he believed to be a young gypsy girl begging in the courtyard. Dripping wet and wringing her white, shrivelled hands, the girl was in obvious distress. As soon as Colonel Lowther spoke to her, however, she vanished before his eyes. Chroniclers of this tale have identified Colonel Lowther's phantom visitor both as the starving Grace Naylor and as the fifteenth-century victim of rape and murder.

Andrew Green in *Ghosts of Today* writes that the 'ghost of a woman often seen near the moat' appeared on 14 March 1979 to 'two highly reputable witnesses' within yards of the East Gate. Mr R.H. Tucker, one of the astronomers at The Royal Observatory headquartered in the grounds at the time, told Green that Mrs Daisy Guy and Mrs Marjorie Haylor, both of Eastbourne, had attended a dance and were leaving in their car through the East Gate at about 10.15 that evening. As the ladies waited for the automatic gate barrier to lift, they suddenly glimpsed a woman wearing a grey, flowing skirt. She crossed the drive from behind a large tree on their right and then passed through two cars at the front of the queue of vehicles waiting to leave. The mysterious woman continued gliding across the grass, only to disappear when she reached the beech hedgerow bordering the grounds.

Mrs Haylor noticed that at one point the figure bent down as if to pick something up before continuing her walk. The witnesses were convinced that she was a flesh-and-blood person, and were horrified when the car in front of them suddenly moved through the gateway. Worried that the grey-clad woman had been run down, Mrs Guy left her car, expecting to find an injured or dead body lying in the hedgerow. She was perhaps even more shocked to find no one there at all.

According to Green, a former colleague of Mr Tucker claimed that whereas the apparition of a man had been seen several times near the East Gate, a 'woman in white' was traditionally believed to haunt the area between the castle gardens and the West Gate near Herstmonceux Church, where Grace Naylor is buried. Green suggests that Grace was, in fact, the grey-clad phantom seen by Mrs Guy and Mrs Haylor, and that the male ghost observed beside the East Gate was that of a man who used to live in one of the lodgekeepers' cottages (since demolished) that were built either side of the gateway. The male phantom, wearing an old-fashioned, long overcoat, appears to be waiting for a lift, but disappears whenever anyone draws close to him (London: Kaye & Ward, 1980, 39-40).

Besides Grace Naylor and the young girl who tried to swim the moat, there is a third woman who might qualify as the White Lady. This is none other than Georgiana Hare Naylor, whose father-in-law, Robert Hare, inherited the castle in a dilapidated state. At his wife's urging, and after consulting with an architect who declared that repairing the structure would be too expensive, Robert Hare demolished the castle interior in 1776 and re-used the materials to build a more modern house in the grounds. From this time until Colonel Lowther began his restoration in the early twentieth century, the castle was uninhabited, a factor which surely contributed to the rise of spooky tales on the estate.

Another factor must have been the eccentric appearance and behaviour of Georgiana Hare Naylor, who, according to her grandson, the writer Augustus Hare, was 'as peculiar as she was beautiful'. An accomplished linguist, she insisted on her family conversing in Greek during meals, and every day, dressed in white, she rode on a white ass to drink from a mineral spring in the park. A tame white doe ran alongside her, accompanying her even to church, where it rested at the end of her pew. One day, at the gate of the park near the church, this beloved white doe was killed by dogs. The broken-hearted Georgiana left Herstmonceux at once and never returned, and in 1807 her husband, Francis Hare Naylor, sold the estate.

According to Judy Middleton, the White Lady is clearly Georgiana, still clad in her long cloak and still riding the grounds of the castle on a white ass, followed by her white doe. Writer Peter Underwood claims that the spectre of

Georgiana seems to saunter in and out of deserted rooms of the castle, having returned in death to the place she so loved in life.

Yet another ghostly relative of the Hare family, dressed in eighteenth-century sailor's clothing and sporting a pigtail, is said to have been seen crawling along the battlements. This phantom is most likely the same one described in Augustus Hare's *The Story of My Life*, when the writer tells of a strange event that occurred some time after 1859. Augustus was in London visiting his eldest brother Francis, who asked if the family had had an ancestor or relation who had gone to India and died there. Augustus denied knowing of any, but Francis insisted that such a person must have existed. Then he related an uncanny experience he had had during a visit to the family home at Herstmonceux Castle.

Intending to spend the night, he had fallen asleep in the high tower by the gateway, and in a vision, he was approached by the figure of a man wearing a pigtail and eighteenth-century dress. The man told Francis that he was a near relation, and that he had come to inform him that even though everyone believed him to have been a poor man while living in India, he had in fact been very rich. If any relatives made inquiries, the man told Francis, they might inherit the fortune themselves.

Augustus denied that the story could be true, as he knew of no family member with any connection to India. Later, however, he learned of the existence of a great-uncle, George Hare, who had moved to India and was believed to have been very rich. When he died, however, there was no word of any inheritance, and it was said by some that he had left no money. Augustus Hare goes on to say that it was entirely possible that this great-uncle had died in possession of a fortune after all, but that no one in the family was able to travel so far away in order to check out the story, so that the subject was eventually dropped.

After the Hare family departed Herstmonceux, the estate had a succession of owners, but the castle continued to fall into ruin until it was purchased by Colonel Lowther in 1911. In addition to the wraith of the dripping girl with shrivelled hands, Colonel Lowther is said to have had another shocking encounter with a ghost, this time while he was out riding his horse. Peter Underwood writes that as the colonel approached the old bridge over the moat, the apparition of a man suddenly came into view, wearing a velvet jacket and riding breeches. Not heeding Colonel Lowther or even seeming to be aware of his presence, the figure stumbled along like a sleepwalker, coming closer and closer until he passed right through the horse's head. Then he disappeared. Was this the apparition of Thomas Fiennes, the third Lord Dacre, who was executed in the sixteenth century? Such an identification seems possible, although the clothing worn by the ghost suggests that he might date from a later period.

Not deterred by his otherworldly experiences on the estate, Colonel Lowther continued his restoration work until he died in 1929, and successive owners, especially Sir Paul Latham, continued to reconstruct the castle. During the Second World War, an insurance society, the Hearts of Oak Friendly Society, evacuated to the estate from London in order to assist the Ministry of Pensions. In 1946 the property was purchased by the Admiralty to be the new home of The Royal Greenwich Observatory until the late 1980s, when the Observatory moved to Cambridge University. Then in 1993 Herstmonceux Castle was purchased by Queen's University at Kingston, Ontario in Canada, to become an international study centre. The castle itself is not open to the public, except for occasional guided tours that are subject to availability. But visitors may wander freely around the grounds and gardens to enjoy one of the most breathtakingly beautiful places in Sussex.

Through its long centuries, and in spite of undergoing so many changes, Herstmonceux Castle has managed to hold on to its sense of history as well as its ghosts. Long may it continue to do so!

Hove Museum
& Art Gallery, Hove, East Sussex

Before the Hove Museum & Art Gallery was opened to the public, it was the private home of one of the town's leading families. Major John Oliver Vallance hired architect Thomas Lainson to design the mansion in an Italianate style made popular by Queen Victoria's Osborne House on the Isle of Wight. The Hove villa, built in 1877, was called Brooker Hall after the Major's father, John Brooker Vallance, who was lord of the manor of Hove in 1867.

The family lived happily in Brooker Hall until Major Vallance died suddenly in 1893, when his children were still minors. Another tragedy hit the Vallances a few years later when the eldest son was killed in a carriage accident. Major Vallance's widow, Emma, continued living in the villa until 1913, and during the First World War she allowed it to be used to house German prisoners of war.

After Emma Vallance's death in the early 1920s, the building was bought by the Hove Corporation for £4000 to be used as a museum. After some refurbishment, it opened to the public on 2 February 1927. In 1966 when Hove Town Hall burned down, the offices of this institution moved for several years into the former Brooker Hall, but it was in use as a museum once more by March 1974.

Most of the unexplained phenomena in the Hove Museum & Art Gallery seem to date from the 1980s onwards. One morning in the early to mid-1980s, a former caretaker, Les Whitehead, was having a talk in the staff room with Terry Sharp, at that time a supervisor. The men abruptly halted their conversation when they heard the distinct sound of footsteps hurrying along the staff passage towards the rear of the museum. Knowing that they were the only ones who should have been in the building at the time, they feared an intruder, but when they got up to search, they found no one.

Several chroniclers have written about the incident, and Judy Middleton, in her *Ghosts of Sussex*, claims that this was not the only time when inexplicable footsteps had been heard, although, she says, they were reported more frequently downstairs (Newbury, Berkshire: Countryside Books, 1988, 52-54). According to Middleton, the sound of a door closing had often accompanied the sound of footsteps passing down an entrance hall corridor that once led to domestic quarters. She points out also that the former breakfast area that later served as the curator's room often felt cold, and that the caretaker's large dog, a Doberman/Great Dane mix, frequently refused to enter it. Even stranger, Middleton claims that a previous caretaker reported that objects were sometimes discovered to have moved from place to place, seemingly on their own.

These strange goings-on piqued the interest of psychic researchers who brought along special equipment to investigate the property in January 1985. Unfortunately, they heard no unexplained footsteps, but when they examined a large embroidered crucifixion scene dating from around 1550, their equipment showed a temperature rise of two degrees on the area of the tapestry representing the body of Christ. Similarly, their ozone-sniffing equipment made a bleeping sound whenever it approached that part of the embroidery. Middleton wonders whether the strange reactions of the equipment could be attributed to the type of wool used for that particular section of the tapestry, but she admits that the incident was strange, nevertheless. She goes on to relate another odd occurrence, in which two girls who were looking at the tapestry left in a hurry, explaining that they felt strange vibrations in the room.

Current supervisor Joan Carey, whom I interviewed in October 2004, reported a strange experience of her own one afternoon in 1989. 'We had a Victorian painters' exhibition on,' she recalled, 'and we'd done up the temporary exhibition galleries as Victorian drawing rooms. The front bay windows, which are normally boarded up, had a mural painted on them, so that spectators had the illusion that they were looking out into the grounds from the drawing room. At the end of the day we go around and lock up, but if there are people still in the galleries, we try not to harass them but to subtly let them know that it's time to go.'

As Joan made her walk through the exhibitions, she noticed a woman standing, apparently looking at the mural. Joan walked on through to the other galleries, which were empty. When Joan walked through the first gallery again, she noticed that the woman was still there.

'I gave my keys a little tinkling sound and then went to stand outside the door in the hall,' she explained. 'I thought that the minute the woman came out, I'd race in there and lock up. But nobody ever came out, and my colleague eventually came down to ask why I wasn't locking the downstairs. I told her that someone was still inside, so we finally went to look. There was no one there. My colleague and I just looked at each other.'

'No one could have left without my knowing it, because I had been standing at the only exit,' Joan insisted. 'I don't believe in ghosts, and even now I don't know if I've seen one, but this was very strange.'

Because Joan was trying to be subtle and unobtrusive at the time, she didn't allow herself to get a good look at the woman, but she believed that the figure was wearing a long grey dress. 'It seemed that she was wearing a grey top with the waist nipped in a bit and a long skirt,' Joan remembered. 'The experience wasn't creepy at the time, because I thought it was a real person. It's not until a while afterwards, when you think, well, if there wasn't anybody in there, whom or what did I see?'

Joan Carey has never known the identity of the figure she saw, but if it was indeed a ghost, it might have been that of Sarah Vallance, wife of John Brooker Vallance and the mother of Major Vallance, the builder of the house. According to John Rackham's *Brighton Ghosts, Hove Hauntings*, Sarah is believed by many to haunt the house, and several of those who have seen a female ghost report that she looks a lot like the image of Sarah in a painting (Brighton: Latimer Publications, 2001, 254-56).

Former caretaker Dennis Parkinson and his wife were among those who witnessed the ghost believed to be Sarah Vallance. For a time they lived in the top flat on the premises, but then they eventually moved out and Mr Parkinson died. Joan Carey recalled that Mrs Parkinson returned to the museum one day and told her about the time she and her husband had seen the phantom.

'She said that as they were coming in one day, going up the stairs, they saw a woman on the top landing. She was wearing fancy dress. The Parkinsons clutched each other in shock, and when they looked again, the woman had gone.'

The flat inhabited by the Parkinsons has since been converted to museum use, but in 1988 previously mentioned caretaker Les Whitehead was living there with his wife and stepdaughter. That year, John Rackham writes, a friend of Mr Whitehead was staying overnight, and just before falling asleep, he was shocked to see a woman come into his room and walk about a while before finally leaving. The light in the room was dim, so the guest presumed that the figure was Mrs Whitehead, who had perhaps come to get something out of the room. The woman had not made any noise, but the man attributed that to her not wanting to wake him.

The next morning at breakfast the guest made a joke about his nocturnal visitor, but no one in the family seemed to know what he was talking about. When he told them what had happened, no one would admit to having been in his room the night before.

Joan Carey recalled for me a nocturnal visit on another occasion, presumably by the same ghost. This incident involved the young friend of Mr Whitehead's stepdaughter, Lisa, who had also come for a sleepover at the flat. Both girls were in Lisa's bedroom, and in the morning the friend asked Lisa, 'Why did your mother keep coming in and looking at us in the night? It kept waking me up.' When Lisa asked her mother the same question, the older woman claimed that she had stayed in her own bed all night. In both Rackham's and Middleton's accounts of this event, the motherly ghost was said to have tucked in the young visitor.

Is it likely that any such proper, maternally concerned phantom would go in for something as mischievous as bottom pinching? Perhaps not, but who else could have been responsible for what happened to a painter who was working by himself at the back of the museum on the north-west side? According to Judy Middleton, the man was engrossed in his work when he suddenly felt himself being pinched. He was shocked to say the least, but even more so when he turned around to find nobody there! He was so unnerved that he rushed out, his work unfinished, and refused to return.

Visitors to the Hove Museum & Art Gallery today might not be so lucky (or unlucky, depending upon how they view such things) as to be pinched or even tucked in by a ghost. They probably won't even hear any unexplained footsteps, but they are guaranteed, at least, an entertaining and enlightening day out.

Jack and Jill Windmills

DUNCTON DOWN, NEAR CLAYTON, WEST SUSSEX

Jack and Jill Windmills are a vision in black and white set into the green rolling downs of the Sussex landscape. They look as if they have stood there since the beginning of time, as if they sprang like trees from the earth below. It's impossible to think of one without the other, or to imagine that they were not always paired as they are now in their picturesque location above the village of Clayton.

Yet they were constructed years and miles apart. Jill, originally called Lashmar's New Mill, is a white post mill built in 1821 in Dyke Road in Brighton. The land she stood on was eventually needed for the growing town's redevelopment, so in about 1852 she was dismantled into sections, which were then hauled by teams of oxen pulling a trolley sledge to her current position on Duncton Down. Here she kept company with the old Duncton post mill until 1866, when Duncton's upper section was dismantled and Jack, a brick tower mill, was built on the site.

Both mills stopped their working lives around 1906, but they probably weren't known by their current names until the late 1920s, when day trippers taking the train from London to Brighton dubbed them 'Jack and Jill'. Jack is now privately owned, but Jill was restored by enthusiasts in 1986 and is open to the public.

The events causing the ghost stories occurred after the mills began to be used as residences. In 1908 Edward A. Martin, writer and archaeologist, came to live in Jack for three years and chronicled his experiences in *Life in a Sussex Windmill* (1921). He reported nothing supernatural, but wrote that during the night, 'the silences were almost appalling'. At other times, however, '[t]he mill in fact spoke. Sometimes there was a decided change of wind, and that rather suddenly. Then the groaning would be like a thousand demons let loose.'

In 1910, Minna Cowper Coles Anson, daughter of the designer of the rotating gun turret, came with her husband, Captain Walter Anson, to take over the mills as well as two adjoining cottages. Captain Anson died shortly after the First World War, but Minna continued living in the property for more than forty years, until she died of a respiratory infection.

Henry Longhurst, golf correspondent of the *Sunday Times*, and his wife Claudine came to live on the site in 1953. Soon they realised they were not alone. Frequently they heard a persistent dry cough coming from the room where Minna Anson had suffered her final illness. According to Simon Potter, who runs the Jack and Jill Windmills Society website, the Longhursts originally attributed the coughing sounds to their children, until they realised that they continued even when the room was empty.

The Longhursts were also bewildered by the unexplained ringing of the servants' bells that Captain Anson had installed on the wall of the kitchen in one of the cottages. These bells were connected by wires to various rooms as well as to the Jack windmill. Before the Longhursts had even moved in, Claudine and a builder were startled one day when all six bells began to ring at once. As Judy Middleton in *Ghosts of Sussex* explains, 'It was not a case of hearing things either, because both of them could see the bells moving' (Newbury, Berkshire: Countryside Books, 1998, 20-22). As soon as the bells stopped, Claudine and the builder checked to make sure that no one else was in the cottages. Right afterwards, Middleton writes, 'the builder opened a cupboard door and was startled to see an old broom zoom out at him, travelling fast and several inches off the ground'.

Another episode with the bells occurred on the Longhursts' first night at the cottage. Around 3.30 in the morning, Henry was awakened by the sound of a bell ringing in the kitchen. According to John Rackham in *Brighton Ghosts, Hove Hauntings*, Henry got up to investigate and found the third bell from the left still swinging. He tried to follow the wire, but his nerves failed him and he went back to bed. 'When morning came,' Rackham writes, 'he traced the wire to the other cottage and a small room where it terminated with a meagre length of wire hanging from the ceiling' (Brighton: Latimer Publications, 2001, 328-29).

Another, even more alarming incident occurred when Claudine Longhurst and her mother saw a pair of tongs leap by themselves across the fireplace in the granary. From time to time, other objects in the house seemed to disappear and then reappear in different locations.

'Henry said they were aware that there was something in there,' Simon Potter told me. In 1963, the cottages were finally pulled down, but new manifestations centred upon the third floor of the Jack windmill. 'It was converted into a chapel back in the 1920s or 30s,' Simon explained. 'I used to go up there on a fairly regular basis, and almost every time, the Bible on the lectern would be open at a different page. This was very strange, since no one had been up there in the intervening time. And this floor is colder than the floors above and below. We go into the windmill about half a dozen times a year with visitors, and you can feel the change in temperature as you walk through.'

Noel Thomas, whose wife Janet is secretary for the Jack and Jill Windmill Preservation Society, has also witnessed the unexplained coldness, as well as the mysterious page-changing of the Bible in the old chapel. But the strangest experience for him was finding the whole third floor covered with the bodies of Sussex Blue butterflies. 'This is a small butterfly that lives on the Downs,' he said, 'a very bright blue and probably just under an inch across the wingspan. The whole of this floor, but no other floor in the windmill, funnily enough, was absolutely covered with their bodies. Every horizontal surface had them on it, and you had to walk across the floor quite carefully to avoid stepping on them. They were all dead - they'd all obviously lived there for a while and then just died.'

Noel, a technician and engineer, claims to be a sceptic about the supernatural, but the dead butterflies nevertheless gave him an eerie feeling. Simon Potter agrees that the phenomenon is weird, but he's seen it elsewhere. 'Windmills seem to attract butterflies like that,' he said. 'It's not unique to Jack - I was over in Anglesey last week, looking at a windmill there, and again we found them. I think they get in during the winter months, and then just perish. It's a shame, because they can't make their way out again.'

The butterflies, perhaps, had no choice about remaining at the windmill. But the same apparently can't be said about the spirit of Minna Anson, or whoever haunts the picturesque location on Duncton Down. That ghost clearly stays because it feels at home.

Knepp Castle
NEAR WEST GRINSTEAD, WEST SUSSEX

Knepp Castle, at least the little that remains of it nowadays, may look for all the world like a nineteenth-century folly, but in its heyday it was a grand family home and fortress, a favourite retreat of royals who used it as a base from which to hunt.

Like the similarly ruined Bramber Castle, Knepp was built by the de Braose family in the twelfth century. In 1210 it was confiscated and partially demolished by King John, who suspected a de Braose plot against him. The castle was then given to one of the king's sons before being restored to the de Braose family after John's death. By the fourteenth century, the castle continued to disintegrate, the process hastened by locals who had no qualms about dismantling its stones for other building work. Further dilapidation continued from the time of Cromwell to the early nineteenth century, when a new Knepp Castle was built just slightly north-west of the old one. The new structure, also built as a private home, was damaged by fire and rebuilt in the early twentieth century, but it is not open to the public.

It is the original Knepp Castle, south of West Grinstead on the main A24 London to Worthing road, which is the setting for one of the most charming and peculiar ghost stories of Sussex.

The legend is that during the days when the castle was held by King John, one of his retainers made advances to a beautiful young girl who rebuffed him. Angered by her refusal to have anything to do with him, the retainer sought out and paid a local witch to turn the unfortunate girl into a white doe. According to the legend, word went around that no one was allowed to harm the lovely animal, but one day, a young man, eager to show off his prowess as a hunter, shot the doe through the heart and killed her.

Since then, the phantom of the white doe has been seen eating grass in the grounds of Knepp Castle, especially around Christmastime. On the spot where she died, red marks that look like blood are said to appear in the snow.

Lamb House
RYE, EAST SUSSEX

Besides attracting ghosts, Lamb House in the charming town of Rye also attracts writers. No fewer than three famous ones have made the eighteenth-century red brick-fronted house their home. And like many of the non-authors who have lived there, too, the writers realised that they were sharing their residence with inhabitants not of this world.

The first and most famous (of the writers, not the ghosts) was American novelist Henry James, who lived at Lamb House from 1897 to 1916. Even before James had moved in, Lamb House had a strange hold over him. He wrote to a friend that he felt 'coerced by some supernatural power that relieves me of all the botheration of a decision or an alternative. I feel absolutely foredoomed to take a lease.' Foredoomed or not, James continued under the strange spell of Lamb House as he began to write his own most chilling ghost story, *The Turn of the Screw*, shortly after moving in.

According to the National Trust, which now owns and administers the house through resident caretakers, James was also said to have seen the phantom of an old woman wearing a mantilla. The woman's identity was unknown, but she was supposed to have helped James with his writing. Apparently no one else has ever seen her, but an amateur photographer once took a photo of Lamb House and was said to have found on the negative an impression of an elderly lady wearing just such a head covering. Unfortunately, no one at the National Trust knows the origins of the story or what happened to the photographic negative. In addition to seeing the woman in the mantilla, James claimed to have felt a mysterious presence at Lamb House.

The next writer to live there, E.F. Benson, was even more susceptible to its otherworldly inhabitants. Best known for his stories about Miss Mapp and Lucia, Benson was also a prodigious writer of ghost stories, certainly inspired at least in part by the time he spent at Lamb House after the death of Henry James.

Benson was especially aware of an unusual atmosphere emanating from the walled or 'secret' garden, and he described it in his *Final Edition: Informal Autobiography*. It was, he writes, 'as if something out of the past, some condition of life long vanished, was leaking through into the present'. At least half a dozen of his friends, he insists, were also aware of this curious blending of the past and present at Lamb House. 'Then,' he continues, 'this atmosphere became more personal: there was somebody there. The presence was in no way perilous or malign, like the presences in the enchanted woods of Ware, nor was it friendly: it was entirely indifferent.'

But then on one hot, still summer day, Benson saw an apparition. He and two friends, including the Vicar of Rye, had had lunch at Lamb House and afterwards strolled down to the secret garden. They were sitting in the shade, close to an open door in the wall that connected to another part of the garden. Benson's and the vicar's chairs were facing the doorway.

'And I saw the figure of a man walk past this open doorway,' Benson writes. 'He was dressed in black and he wore a cape the right wing of which, as he passed, he threw across his chest, over his left shoulder. His head was turned away and I did not see his face. The glimpse I got of him was very short, for two steps took him past the open doorway, and the wall behind the poplars hid him again.'

The vicar jumped up, exclaiming, 'Who on earth was that?' The men hurried through the open door to see where their mysterious intruder had gone, but the garden was empty. When Benson and the vicar compared notes as to what they had seen, it became clear that they had witnessed the same thing. The only difference was that the vicar noticed that the phantom was wearing hose.

Benson puzzled for a long time over the experience and what it had meant. A short time later the vicar again saw the apparition in broad daylight at exactly the same spot. Benson was with him, but this time saw nothing. 'Since then I think I have seen it once in the evening on the lawn near the garden-room,' he writes, 'but it was dusk, and I may have construed some fleeting composition of light and shadow into the same figure' (London: Longmans Green and Co., 1940, 257-59).

Benson wrote that, at the time of the sightings, there was no ghostly legend about any such cloaked figure at Lamb House that would have predisposed anyone to imagine seeing it. But Rumer Godden, the writer who lived at Lamb House after Benson, believed that the apparition was that of Allen Grebell, whose murder on 17 March 1743 had shocked and horrified Rye.

At that time, the Lambs were one of the most prominent families in the town. James Lamb had built Lamb House in 1723, and both he and his son went on to serve as Mayor of Rye many times. On the night of the murder, James Lamb had intended to attend a banquet on board a revenue sloop moored by the fishing Salts. But he didn't feel well, and at the very last minute, his brother-in-law Allen Grebell offered to take his place. It was a wet and chilly night, and as Grebell didn't have time to return to his house to put on something warmer, James Lamb loaned him his own red mayoral cloak.

Around midnight, Grebell was returning from the banquet, taking a shortcut through the churchyard. John Breads, a butcher, lay in wait, and seeing the red mayoral cloak, he lurched out and stabbed Grebell twice in the back. Not realising the extent of his injuries, Grebell staggered back to his own home opposite Lamb House. He explained to his servant that a drunken man had fallen against him on the way home, and as he felt a little shaken by the incident, he wanted to stay up for a while in front of the fire before retiring to bed.

Across the way at Lamb House, James Lamb was himself having a disturbed night. Three times he dreamed that his deceased wife had returned to say, 'James, I am very alarmed about Allen. Get up and see if he is all right.' Twice James woke, only to go back to sleep. At dawn, he roused himself to walk over to Grebell's house, only to find that his brother-in-law had died during the night. Accounts differ as to whether Grebell was found by his servant or by Lamb, but what is clear is that he was found in his chair in a pool of blood, having bled to death from an unsuspected stab wound.

At first Grebell's servant was suspected of the murder, but then someone reported having seen the butcher John Breads dancing in the streets, drunkenly proclaiming that 'Butchers should kill lambs'. Subsequently, a butcher's knife covered with blood, and with the name 'Breads' on the handle, was discovered in the churchyard.

The insane Breads was found guilty. Before sentencing him, Mayor James Lamb asked him if he had anything to say. 'I did not mean to kill Mr Grebell,' Breads blurted out. 'It was you I meant it for, and I would murder you now if I could.' Breads had apparently killed Grebell, mistaking him for Lamb, as revenge for Lamb's having fined Breads six years earlier for selling short-weight meat.

Breads was hanged just outside Rye, and his corpse was tarred to preserve it. Then the remains were placed inside an iron cage and hung from the gallows on Gibbetts Marsh. When the flesh eventually rotted away and the bones fell to the ground, they were eagerly snatched by witches, who believed them to have magical powers. The iron cage and Breads' skull are still kept as grisly artefacts in the Town Hall.

Rumer Godden never saw the apparition of Breads' victim, Allen Grebell, or any other during her tenure at Lamb House, but the novelist did believe herself to be plagued by a poltergeist there. Writing in her autobiography, *A House with Four Rooms,* she claimed that the troublesome spirit came to bother her in her first weeks as a tenant at Lamb House. She had the old-fashioned kitchen renovated, and although the renovation had charm, she wrote, apparently the 'presences' in the house objected to it, causing the new boiler and new pipes to burst, saucepans to be hurtled off their shelves, and 'electricity fused'. The situation got so bad that she called in a priest to perform an exorcism. 'He even blessed the refrigerator,' she wrote, adding that afterwards there 'was a sudden lull, then peace' (London: Macmillan, 1989, 265-66).

The poltergeist never again made such a huge nuisance of itself, but it continued to play tricks. Godden left a few pages of a manuscript on a table in the Green Study and then took her dog for a walk. Returning after lunch, she found the pages gone, but no one in the house would admit to taking them. A thorough search was made, but still they were not found. Two days later, upon entering her study in the morning, Godden found the missing pages on the desk.

Another time, she recalled writing 'The End' and the date to finish off a long project. She laid down her pen, and at that moment, the pen split in two from top to bottom (285-86).

Like both James and Benson before her, Rumer Godden often felt that 'presences' haunted Lamb House, although one wonders whether she wasn't merely being fanciful when she decided that these spirits were those of Miles and Flora, the child characters from Henry James' *The Turn of the Screw.* The notion that James' fictional characters had somehow materialised into 'presences' in the house came after a visit of Godden's own four grandchildren.

'I realise that for more than a hundred years there has not been a child at Lamb House,' she writes. 'Now suddenly Lamb House was alive with those shrill, sometimes piercing child voices, scampering of feet'. Sometimes, amidst the chaos of the children at play, she felt 'a strange sense of "presences", two other children, silent, well-behaved. It was as if they were watching. Soon I knew who they were, Miles and Flora'. Her own grandchildren, she explains, had brought the fictional children out of the Green Study where Henry James had conceived them, and after 'her four' had gone, Miles and Flora remained (280).

Miles and Flora may no longer be at Lamb House, but the current resident caretakers believe that the poltergeist who troubled Rumer Godden is still about. Sue Harris and Tony Davis have lived at Lamb House since 2000, and they, too, have had things go missing, only to mysteriously reappear.

'I lost the top to a pen,' Sue told me, 'and I found it about three months later, just lying on the fireplace hearth in the dining room, where we couldn't possibly have missed seeing it. And once we couldn't find the key to the courtyard door. We hunted all over, but couldn't find it anywhere. Later that evening, I went out into the courtyard, and there was the key, lying on the cobbles. Again, we couldn't have missed it earlier if it had been there.'

Still another key went missing, only to turn up again months later - this time inside the cupboard where the burglar alarm is installed! 'We get into that cupboard twice a day,' Sue said, 'but one day, after all that time, we found the key just lying inside.'

Even stranger was an episode during the Christmas holidays of 2003, when Sue's daughter's boyfriend and his sister were visiting. 'The sister was staying in what had been one of the servants' rooms on the top floor,' Sue explained. 'She asked my daughter whether I'd been tidying her clothes. I hadn't even been into her room, but somebody, and it wasn't any of us, had folded her clothes up and put them back neatly into her suitcase!'

'When she told me, I said that she must have done it and forgotten about it, but she just laughed and said, "Believe me - I never fold up my clothes!" The interesting thing about this is that she was, after all, staying in what had been the maids' quarters.'

Sue recalled another time when friends were looking after the house while she and Tony were away. 'We thought it would be a great privilege for them to stay in the guest bedroom, the room where George I once stayed,' she said. 'It's a lovely room, absolutely gorgeous, looking up to the church and over the garden. But they stayed there only once and refuse to stay there again. Another friend says that she feels a presence in that room, although we don't feel it ourselves.'

Could this ghostly presence be that of George I himself? The royal visit Sue alludes to occurred when the king was returning from his beloved Hanover. A ferocious storm blew his ship onto nearby Camber Sands, and he was rescued and taken to Lamb House by a group of Rye townsmen led by Mayor James Lamb. That same night, James' wife Martha gave birth to the couple's fourth child, a son who was of course named George. The king was pleased to become the child's godfather and presented his new namesake with an inscribed silver bowl.

The presence felt by Sue and Tony's friends may well have been that of the king, as he was reportedly sighted by a previous tenant. Jane Fraser Hay, a Blue Badge guide, told me that the tenant had told her that she had seen the apparition of the king sitting in a chair in a corner of the room he had occupied.

Another ghost sitting in a chair was reported by Andrew Green in *Haunted Sussex Today* (Seaford, East Sussex: S.B. Publications, 1997, 71). Green claimed that an old woman wearing Victorian clothing had been seen in a corner chair in the hall next to the front door, and that many visitors had wondered who she was and why she disappeared so suddenly. Green went on to say that Rumer Godden had implied that the ghost might have been that of Henry James' cook, Mrs Paddington.

The lovely Lamb House in Rye continues to attract its fair share both of ghosts and of writers. The late novelist Joan Aiken, herself a Rye native, provided a fictional treatment of James' and Benson's encounters with the strange phenomena at the property in *The Haunting of Lamb House*, published in 1991. Strangely enough, however, none of the writers who lived at Lamb House is believed to haunt their old home, although Henry James' ghost has been said to haunt the Lenox, Massachusetts home of his close friend, the novelist Edith Wharton. James' phantom has been seen in a second-floor hallway, chatting away to another ghost who closely resembles Wharton herself. Edith Wharton visited Lamb House when Henry James lived there, so perhaps they could be persuaded, along with E. F. Benson and Rumer Godden, to come along and join the other phantoms once again at the elegant Georgian house in Rye.

Lewes Castle

LEWES, EAST SUSSEX

Built only a decade or so after the Battle of Hastings, the imposing Lewes Castle is a glorious reminder of some of the earliest days of recorded Sussex history. William de Warenne, the first Earl of Surrey, constructed the castle to defend the vital crossing over the nearby River Ouse, and further additions to the fortifications were made in the thirteenth and fourteenth centuries. The castle was attacked only once, during the Battle of Lewes on 14 May 1264, when Simon de Montfort and his barons defeated Henry III. As a result, they were able to impose conditions on the king that are now regarded as the first steps toward parliamentary democracy in England.

It is perhaps surprising that such an ancient and significant building should have so few tales of the supernatural associated with it. And of those, the most famous is almost certainly untrue.

This is the legend related by many authors, most recently by John Rackham in his *Brighton Ghosts, Hove Hauntings,* in which the Earls de Warenne were battling the Lords of Pevensey on the slopes of Mount Caburn just outside Lewes (Brighton: Latimer Publications, 2001, 60-62). The wife of the Earl de Warenne watched the battle from the turret of Lewes Castle, clutching her first-born son in her arms. As the battle drew to its climax, she was horrified to see Lord Pevensey, mounted on his steed with his battle-axe raised and ready to

strike, heading straight for her husband.

In response, Lady de Warenne lifted her child above her head and began praying to St Nicholas, the protector of the faithful in danger. She vowed that if the saint spared her husband's life, their son would not marry until he had travelled to Byzantium. There, on the tomb of the Virgin Mary, he would offer up a treasure acquired by the de Warennes, the belt worn by St Nicholas himself.

St Nicholas apparently heard Lady de Warenne's prayer. Her husband avoided the attack by Lord Pevensey, who was caught off balance and almost fell from his horse. The Earl de Warenne was thus able to stab and mortally wound Lord Pevensey, thus winning the battle.

Every year the de Warenne victory over Lord Pevensey was celebrated at Lewes Castle, and at the twentieth anniversary festivities, the de Warenne heir Manfred, grown to adulthood, took the hand of his fiancée, Lady Edona, and led her to join in the dancing. Suddenly an icy wind swept through the hall, extinguishing the brightly burning candles and torches, while lightning flashed all about. But instead of thunder, the assembled guests heard the sounds of the battle that had taken place twenty years before, and upon the castle's tapestries they saw played out the final fight between Lord Pevensey and the Earl de Warenne. But this time, just as Lord Pevensey raised his battle-axe to strike, the eerie sights and sounds faded away and the inside of the hall was as black as midnight.

The Earl de Warenne took the strange events as an omen, and the next day he travelled to Brighthelmstone (Brighton) to ask the priests at St Bartholomew's Chapel what to do. They advised him to build a ship to send Manfred to the Blessed Virgin's tomb in Byzantium. Until he had fulfilled his mother's promise to St Nicholas, the young man could never be allowed to marry.

According to the legend, Manfred departed from what is now Newhaven and sailed to Byzantium. A year passed, and on 17 May, a ship carrying the pennant of St Nicholas was observed off the coast of Wordinges, known today as Worthing. The de Warenne family, along with Lady Edona, were alerted that Manfred was returning, and they all gathered on the hill next to St Nicholas' Church in Brighthelmstone. There they sang hymns of joyful thanksgiving as the ship approached.

But then, as the ship came ever closer, the watchers couldn't believe their eyes. Without warning, the vessel suddenly keeled over and sank, after colliding with a hidden rock near Shoreham. Lady Edona was so distraught that she collapsed to the ground and died instantly of shock.

Shattered by his son's death, the Earl de Warenne built a new St Nicholas' Church on the very spot where the crowd had gathered to watch the return of Manfred's ship. Lady Edona was buried where she fell, in a spot close to the entrance to the church. According to the legend, on 17 May of each year, anyone standing on the hill by the church will be able to see the final moments of Manfred's doomed ship.

John Rackham points out that as much as we might want to believe this legend, several problems stand in the way. Notwithstanding the fact that Lady de Warenne must have had incredibly acute eyesight to see a battle being fought about two miles away on Mount Caburn, another, even more insurmountable fact is that the Earl de Warenne of the legend, the last of his line, never sired a child. Another fact is that none of the Earls de Warenne had a son called Manfred, and perhaps most significant of all, the tomb of the Virgin Mary is traditionally believed to be not in Byzantium (now known as Istanbul), but in either the Vale of Kidron or Ephesus.

Rackham says that another part of the legend suggests that Lady Edona is buried at the site of a large cross close to the entrance of St Nicholas' Church. But what remains of the cross, largely destroyed during the Reformation, is now believed to mark the burial of a Saxon warrior and his horse.

The most famous legend associated with Lewes Castle may not be true, but it probably had its uses in past centuries. Undoubtedly those in the smuggling trade told it to would-be watchers to keep them inside their homes when illegal activities were afoot. It's interesting to contrast that attitude with the one today, when ghost stories are more apt to attract the curious than to drive away the intimidated!

Another much better documented tale of the supernatural at Lewes Castle also involves the de Warenne family. In this story, Isabella, countess of Arundel and daughter of William de Warenne, was staying at Lewes Castle when her nephew, the son of Hugh Bigod, became gravely ill. Every day the boy's condition worsened, and doctors were unable to help him. When all hope seemed to be gone, the boy's father left Lewes Castle and asked that funeral preparations be made.

The heartbroken Isabella withdrew to her chapel to pray, asking to be told when her nephew had died. A nurse and several other women of the household gathered around the dying child's bed, and suddenly a girl of noble family, named Johanna, came forward. She began calling on the name of St Richard of Wych, who had baptised the sick boy years before. St Richard, bishop of Chichester from 1244 until his death in 1253, was said to have performed many miracles of healing, and Johanna beseeched him to ask the Virgin Mary to restore the boy to health.

No sooner had she finished speaking than the boy opened his eyes and asked that the Blessed Sacrament be brought to him. When he received it, he was completely healed, without even a trace of illness. This story, originally in Latin, is part of the *Life of St. Richard bishop of Chichester* written by the bishop's contemporary, Ralph Bocking, and recently translated into English for David Jones's *Saint Richard of Chichester: The sources for his life* (Lewes: Sussex Record Society, 1995, 215-16).

Much less well documented (at least by me) is the tale of a spectral woman in white who is supposed to walk Lewes Castle at night. I was unable to locate any information about this phantom, who was apparently the subject of an article in the *Sussex Express* in the nineteenth century. But perhaps a connection exists between this ghost and one seen in Barbican House on the castle grounds.

'My grandparents used to have the job of caretakers to Lewes Castle and lived in accommodation in Barbican House,' Alison Langridge told me. 'I was about six years old, and Grandad had closed up for the day. My mother and grandmother were chatting in the foyer downstairs, and I went off upstairs to explore. I was looking in a display case when a very strange cold descended on me, even though, as I recall, it was summer. This wasn't a normal type of cold. After looking in the display case, I started to descend the stairs, and along the landing a woman was very slowly hovering.

'I can only describe her as looking like a glass etching,' Alison continued. 'Half of her was white and half was transparent. Her eyes were transparent, too. She was wearing a long dress. I watched her for about ten minutes before getting bored, and then went back to my mother and grandmother.

'At the time, I didn't know about ghosts, and I didn't give this experience a great deal of thought, but it always stuck in my mind. A few years after this, when my auntie told me a spooky story and I asked her what a ghost was, she said it was the departed dead. That so scared me that I experienced a delayed fear of the Barbican House apparition. For many years, I was scared of ghosts because I had seen one and believed that they existed.'

The only other Lewes Castle ghost story I was able to find is surely fictional. 'The Spectre-Knight of Lewes Castle', by an unidentified author, was published in 1934 in *The Sussex County Magazine* (Vol. 8, 749-51). An introduction to the story claims that the 'old-fashioned' tale was taken from a copy of the *London Journal* of 26 August 1848, and was being 'presented to Sussex readers in the hope that someone may be able to throw light upon the extraordinary and uncanny happenings that it relates'. Readers are told that no origin of the legend was given, and no author's name was attributed to the story.

The tale describes 'Lord Eustace de Warenne', alone in Lewes Castle on a stormy night at the end of August 1307. He is visited by a 'dark rider', the hellish ghost of his elder brother, a 'tall and martial-looking figure with helm and plume, as arrayed for the battle-field'. This brother's 'unexpected' death had left Eustace with the deceased man's title, position, and bride, and the ghoulish phantom has returned to carry his scheming brother off to hell. An accompanying crash of thunder shakes the ground as a bolt of lightning rents asunder the eastern keep of the castle, crushing Lord Eustace beneath the ruins. The story ends by telling us that 'when, after a lapse of some centuries, a portion of the rubbish was cleared from the spot, the mouldering remains of a skeleton seemed to give colour to the tradition of Lewes Castle'.

Throughout its long history, Lewes Castle may have been the setting or inspiration for only a few tales of the supernatural, true or not, but the quality of the stories is definitely better than most!

Michelham Priory
UPPER DICKER, EAST SUSSEX

ithout a doubt, Michelham Priory is one of the most historic, as well as one of the most haunted places in Sussex. Only a handful of properties in the county can boast of so many phantoms as this former Augustinian Priory, founded in 1229 by Gilbert d'Aquila, whose ancestors hailed from the Norman town of L'Aigle. The Augustinian canons, known as 'black canons' because of the colour of their habit, comprised one of the religious orders of the medieval church. These men were not monks, but ordained priests who lived communally according to the teachings of St Augustine of Hippo, the fourth and fifth-century theologian from North Africa. The Augustinians attempted to balance contemplation and prayer with service to the outside community, which meant that the canons served as priests to local churches and hospitals.

Between five and ten canons, perhaps more in the early days, lived at Michelham, and in addition to their individual duties in the community, they each played a role in the running of the priory, assisted by officials and servants in the manner of a great household. Religious houses also provided food and lodging for travellers from all social classes, and as Michelham Priory lay near an important road leading from Lewes to Battle as well as to the ports of Hastings and Rye, it undoubtedly played host to many visitors, including John Pecham, the Archbishop of Canterbury, in 1283 and King Edward I in 1302.

By the middle of the fifteenth century, however, Michelham Priory was falling into decline and disrepute. The prior was accused of extravagant living and financial irresponsibility, and of failing to keep the buildings in good repair. The canons were blamed for not observing the rules of silence, for not eating together in the rectory, and for drunkenness at the tavern outside the priory gate. One even admitted to an affair with a local married woman.

While the obviously 'dissolute' lives of the canons probably eroded their popular support among locals, such bad behaviour had nothing to do with the 'Dissolution of the Monasteries' instituted by Henry VIII. Caring nothing for the spiritual poverty of the church, the king turned his attention instead to its material riches, which he desperately wanted in order to boost his own coffers and to help pay for defence of the realm. Therefore, by Henry's decree and through the agency of his Secretary of State Thomas Cromwell, all the religious houses of England were closed between 1536 and 1540, and their wealth was confiscated.

When Michelham Priory was dissolved in 1537, most of its eight canons went on to find other employment in the church. The church bells were sold to a Maidstone brazier for £27, while the jewels, silver vessels, and ecclesiastical ornaments were sold for £43. The church and the eastern range were demolished for building materials, while the lead from the roofs was kept for use by the king, who granted the priory's estates to Thomas Cromwell at a low rent. But Cromwell, in spite of being showered with many such rewards for his services, fell from royal favour and was executed in 1540. At that time the estate went back to the Crown, and some of it was leased or sold separately.

From 1556, Michelham Priory served as a Tudor gentleman's residence for a succession of owners who made necessary additions and renovations. Thomas Sackville, later created the Earl of Dorset, bought the property in 1601, and his family owned Michelham Priory for nearly three hundred years. In the seventeenth and eighteenth centuries, however, the Sackvilles leased the estate in separate holdings to various tenants who farmed the land. In 1896, they finally sold the priory to James Eglington Anderson Gwynne, who, although he did not live on the grounds, began a programme of much needed renovation and restoration.

In 1925 the Gwynnes sold Michelham Priory and three hundred forty-one acres to Richard Beresford-Wright, who continued the renovations with the help of an architect and a local builder. On 19 December 1927, however, disaster struck when a fire destroyed much of the Tudor Wing, including the original panelling. Undaunted, the Beresford-Wrights persevered with their restoration not only of the priory buildings but also of the grounds, moving the farm to a new location outside the moat so that the lawns and gardens might be extended. Mr Beresford-Wright had wanted to leave the priory either to the National Trust or the Sussex Archaeological Society, but as he could provide no endowment for its upkeep, when he died in 1951, the property was sold instead to Mrs Joyce Storey.

Mrs Storey went on in 1958 to sell the priory buildings and the moat to Mrs Stella Hotblack, who shared Mr Beresford-Wright's dream of preserving the property for posterity. She made the necessary conversions in order to open Michelham Priory to the public, and with an endowment she received as a memorial to a friend killed in the Second World War, Mrs Hotblack was able to give the priory in trust to the Sussex Archaeological Society on 1 November 1959.

As is true of most historic properties that happen to be haunted, the ghosts at Michelham provide fascinating glimpses into different eras of the estate's colourful past. In fact, the oldest spectre alleged to wander the grounds, that of King Harold on his way to engage with William the Conqueror at Battle, died more than one hundred fifty years before the priory was even built on the site of an earlier manor house. And if the legend is correct that Thomas Becket's first miracle was performed near the Mill House, it, too, occurred long before the priory had been established. According to Andrew Green in *Ghosts of the South East*, Richard d'Aquila, grandfather of priory founder Gilbert, had been taking the young Thomas hunting. While crossing a mill stream, the future Archbishop of Canterbury fell with his horse, and it was only owing to the miraculous closing of the sluice gates that he was not swept to a painful death under the mill wheel (London: David & Charles, 1976, 62).

The extent to which paranormal phenomena were reported at Michelham Priory before the late nineteenth century is not known, but they seem likely to have taken place from the earliest days. And a workman's discovery in 1972 of a seventeenth-century Bellarmine jar provides evidence of a strong belief in occult forces at the priory during that century, at least.

These types of stoneware bottles, produced to store wine or beer, were decorated with a sculpted, caricatured image of the Italian Cardinal Roberto Bellarmino, who lived from 1542-1621. This Jesuit theologian spoke out strongly against both Protestants and sorcery. To return the favour, Protestants were wont to show their disdain by smashing the jugs imprinted with the Cardinal's face, while practitioners of witchcraft often placed ingredients for their spells inside them. Conversely, the so-called 'witch bottles' were also used to deflect such curses. People believing themselves to be under threat from a witch's spell would fill the jugs with the appropriate substances, seal them, and bury them under a hearth or doorstep for protection.

The Bellarmine jar at Michelham Priory, found while workers were digging a trench, contained a number of rusted pins stuck into a darkened lump of some unidentified substance. Judy Middleton in *Ghosts of Sussex* points out that a jar of pins was a well known remedy against evil, but that the inclusion in the bottle of something which might be an animal heart suggests instead that a curse was being laid (Newbury, Berkshire: Countryside Books, 1988, 65-66). Andrew Green in *Ghosts of the South East* writes that the discovery of such an object on the grounds of what had been a religious house provides evidence that witchcraft was actively pursued in the area. This seventeenth-century find, he suggests, might even recall practices of earlier times when local witches cast spells or curses on the prior, or even upon the whole priory, and then buried containers with the heart of a sheep, goat, or perhaps even a newborn child inside, as close to the walls as possible, ensuring that the strength of the curse would be concentrated on a particular part of the house (67-69).

We shall probably never know the full story of witchcraft at Michelham Priory, but it seems unlikely that the charming, affable ghost of the prior who greets visitors near the gatehouse could ever have been the object of a curse himself. Still seen today, this friendly phantom was first reported during the tenure of the Beresford-Wrights, when several friends of the family claimed to have been met at the gatehouse by a pleasant gentleman dressed like an Augustinian prior. This cheerful ghost, with his hair cut to resemble Christ's crown of thorns, smiled and pointed the way, as if directing his guests to visit the priory. According to Andrew Green, the phantom wore a dark cloak, a white underskirt, and open sandals. When the visitors turned round to thank the man, they were shocked to see no trace of him, and when they later related the incident to the Beresford-Wrights, the owners were equally perplexed, having never seen the figure themselves (*Ghosts of the South East*, 66-67).

According to psychic investigator Kathy Gearing of The Ghost Club, the phantom of the prior appears to be so solid that witnesses generally assume him to be a member of staff dressed up for a special occasion. He is widely believed to be John Leem, Michelham's best known prior, who held that office from 1374 to 1417. In addition to his religious duties, Leem was also active in local administration, as he collected rents and served on the commission of sewers for the Pevensey Levels, the body responsible for ensuring proper land drainage. Leem used his position to Michelham's advantage, enlarging the endowment by adding the revenues of the churches of Alfriston and Fletching. He was also responsible for construction of the gatehouse in the late fourteenth century, and writer Judy Middleton points out that because of this, no spirit has a better right to frequent that area than he does (64).

Prior John Leem wasn't the only apparition to make its first known appearance while the Beresford-Wright family owned the priory. For some time following the disastrous fire of 1927, Mr Beresford-Wright found his horses in a terrible state. Covered with sweat and shivering in terror, they kicked frantically at the stable walls, their bodies contorted in agony. Weeks later, when the animals were still behaving in such a disturbed manner, Mr Beresford-Wright went to question a stable boy, who suggested that the cause of the panic might be a huge white stallion that kept entering the stables. Since that time, the spectral stallion has been reported on several occasions and has continued to frighten any horses, especially mares, inside the stables at the time.

The origin of this story apparently dates from 1896, when the Sackville family decided to sell the priory to James Gwynne, the wealthy Midlands industrialist known as 'The Iron Master'. Negotiations with other potential buyers had been going on, and one of them, a prosperous farmer, was outraged that the property had been sold out from under him. John Rackham in *Brighton Ghosts, Hove Hauntings* says that when the arrogant Mr Gwynne arrived to claim his property 'astride a white stallion like some conquering warrior', the enraged farmer lost no time in making his feelings known. The result was that the white stallion was soon galloping riderless into the distance, leaving Mr Gwynne fuming and humiliated on the ground (Brighton: Latimer Publications, 2001, 344).

In addition to the White Stallion and the friendly Prior Leem, at least one other apparition is known to have made an appearance when the Beresford-Wrights were at Michelham Priory. Commonly known as the Grey Lady, this is probably the best known of the priory's ghosts, and the one spotted most often, although, ironically, there is much disagreement as to her identity.

According to Andrew Green, a couple of friends of the Beresford-Wrights were enjoying a quiet walk around the grounds one summer evening when they noticed a woman standing on the bridge in front of the gatehouse. Dressed in a grey gown, the woman had a sad expression on her face as she gazed into the moat beneath her. When the couple later asked their hosts about the identity of 'the other guest', they were assured that they were the only visitors staying at Michelham at that time. Over the next few months other visitors to the priory reported seeing the same sad-looking woman.

His curiosity piqued, Mr Beresford-Wright made some enquiries to try to find out the identity of the mysterious phantom. He learned only that she might have been a member of the Sackville family whose baby daughter was said to have drowned after falling into the water (*Ghosts of the South East*, 67). Writer John Rackham points out that unfortunately, when Mr Beresford-Wright was making these enquiries, he was unaware of a woman named Martha Bates, born in Rye in 1870, who had compiled a private collection of ghost stories she had heard, some of them referring to a grey-clad apparition at Michelham Priory. According to these tales, the stately spectre was seen to walk through a closed door and into one of the bedchambers, where she then moved to a window next to the bed. There she appeared to be watching someone sleep, before shrinking back as if disappointed and then leaving the room (345-46).

Judy Middleton points out that Sussex chronicler Arthur Becket, writing in 1911, told similar tales about the Grey Lady. Becket failed to specify which room the night-walking phantom frequented, but he claimed that sleepers there could expect the apparition, dressed in grey silk, to walk to the bed, draw aside the curtain, and gaze at the occupant for a minute or two before walking away in disappointment, her silk dress making a rustling sound (Middleton, 64-65).

If we assume, perhaps incorrectly, that only one Grey Lady haunts Michelham Priory, we may wonder why the more recent tales place her outdoors rather than indoors, in daylight hours rather than in the evening, and why she is now often accompanied by a small dog, usually described as a brown or black and white terrier.

The most frequently related occurrence took place on a summer day in the early 1970s, when a thin and very ill-looking woman dressed in grey approached the ticket kiosk in the gatehouse. With her was a small black and white dog. When the attendant realised that the woman had the animal with her, he informed her that pets were not allowed. The woman, however, glided along as if she hadn't heard and moved on past a couple of other visitors waiting for tickets. Unable to catch up with the woman in grey, the attendant believed that she would later be stopped by one of the guides.

The couple waiting for admittance, described conflictingly by various writers as either middle-aged or elderly, then passed through the gateway themselves. The woman turned to her husband to comment upon the unusual dress worn by the woman who had so rudely brushed past them without paying for a ticket. The man, puzzled, asked his wife whom she was talking about, as he had seen no one. In answer, the wife looked again toward the woman and the dog, and as she gazed, the two figures disappeared.

The incident so unnerved the couple that both had to be given first aid. The kiosk attendant had also seen the phantom vanish into thin air, but apparently he was better able to take the experience in his stride. Since then, several others have claimed to see the Grey Lady and her dog in the same vicinity, and she is still observed gazing mournfully from the bridge in front of the gateway. In some versions of the tale, she turns back when told that dogs are not allowed in the grounds, only to disappear along the driveway. R. Moore, in *Sussex Ghosts*, writes that the Grey Lady prefers to do her haunting in the twilight hours, and that she has been seen 'straddling the moat' (St Ives, Cornwall: James Pike Ltd, 1976, 13-14). In the 1980s, according to John Rackham, the same busy ghost was seen chasing her dog across the lawn at the rear of the priory before fading away as she reached a door of the building (347).

Judy Middleton believes it unlikely that the Grey Lady is a member of the Sackville family, who, even though they owned Michelham Priory for nearly three hundred years, lived elsewhere and rented the property to tenants, including three generations of the Child family from 1791 to 1861. Middleton believes that the Grey Lady may instead be the mother of a five-year-old boy, Robert Child, who was said to have died in a tragic accident at the priory. The story is that while he was playing in the nearby watermill, his clothing became entangled by the wheel of the machine used for dressing the flour, and he was strangled (64-65).

Oddly, another and better-documented tragedy involving the Child family also involves a drowning. According to a report in the *Sussex Weekly Advertiser* dated 3 September 1798, a shepherd in the service of a Mr Child of Michelham was drowned as a result of a wager for a bottle of gin. Attempting to wade around the circumference of the moat, the man lost his footing, and none of the fellow servants who were also present could save him (R. Stevens-Bassett, *Ghostly Tales & Hauntings of East Sussex*, CLX, 1993, 17).

In one version of the Grey Lady stories, the disconsolate phantom is said to gaze down into the moat where she herself, rather than her child, fell in and drowned. This version sounds as if it might be a confused composite of the others, and it's doubtful whether anyone will ever discover what truth may underlie the Grey Lady tales.

Likewise, it's also difficult to identify the ghosts of a man and a Blue Lady who appear occasionally in the Tudor room, which had to be reconstructed after the fire of 1927. Andrew Green writes that the first known sighting of this eerie pair was in the early 1970s, just a few weeks after the Grey Lady so disconcerted the couple waiting for tickets at the gatehouse. In this incident, however, a young couple from overseas were reading the notices on the walls about the objects and details of the Tudor room. When at one point they turned around to study an object more closely, they were astonished to see a middle-aged man in a cloak descending from the ceiling in a diagonal direction! When he was nearly to the level of the floor in front of the inglenook fireplace, he appeared to jump silently as if from an invisible step. Then he continued his silent, quick glide through the end doorway.

Before the young couple could do more than gaze at each other in shock, dismayed that no one else in the room appeared to have seen the apparition, along came another one - the figure of a middle-aged woman in a Tudor gown suddenly hurried out of the farthest room at the western end. She rushed past the couple as if she were chasing the man, who had by this time vanished.

Intrigued, the visitors told the custodian what they had seen, and asked whether a staircase might once have descended into the room where the fireplace now stands. His answer was that even though there was no record of an original staircase, such a thing was certainly possible. It might even have been an external one, he explained, and thus the woman who chased the man might originally have been in the garden (*Ghosts of the South East*, 70-71).

Green's *Ghosts of the South East* was published in 1976, the same year that R. Moore published *Sussex Ghosts*. Moore's descriptions of the ghosts in the Tudor room differ markedly from Green's, however. According to Moore, the male and female phantoms had 'often turned up in the afternoon during visiting hours', and the male was dressed in a 'medieval costume similar to that worn by Augustinian canons who built the priory'. His female phantom, on the other hand, is described as a 'lady in blue'. Also in contrast to Green, Moore says that both figures 'walked through the wall, down some stairs that were not there in the first place, crossed to the far end of the hall, turned and finally walked out of an open front door'. According to Moore, the 'lady in blue stalked into a large room, then a smaller one, before revealing herself, and finally disappeared through the outer stone wall'. He adds that visitors from Seaford claimed to have seen both phantoms walk through inner walls as well as the outer wall of the priory (13-14).

Are Green and Moore writing about the same pair of phantoms whose clothing has been perceived differently by various witnesses, or could two separate couples, one from the Tudor era and the other from the medieval period, be haunting the priory? If the latter assumption is true, and we assume that these particular spectres are not actually spirits but rather visual phenomena resulting from psychic impressions upon the environment, it may be difficult to explain how or why medieval ghosts would appear in a part of the priory that didn't exist during their lifetimes.

Judy Middleton, publishing *Ghosts of Sussex* in 1988, tells much the same story as Andrew Green, adding that no one seems to have noted the style or colour of the Tudor-era gown worn by the female ghost as she hurried after the man in the black cloak (65). Middleton makes no mention of a Blue Lady or a ghostly canon frequenting this part of the priory. If there is any hope of solving the mystery, then, it seems that we will have to wait for further, more detailed incidents to be reported.

The builders of the Tudor wing where these phantoms have been sighted have themselves made an appearance. According to Kathy Gearing, the ghosts of Herbert Pelham and his wife, who bought the priory in 1587, have been seen on the premises; and Thomas Sackville, to whom the Pelhams sold the property in 1601, has been both seen and heard.

Apparitions from a later era have also been witnessed, according to John Rackham, who writes that a small group of visitors and their guide standing close to the foot of the main staircase once watched the descent of two ladies in Edwardian dress. These phantoms proceeded nonchalantly down the stairs and then walked towards a garden exit before vanishing. Rackham notes that as this staircase was built after the fire of 1927 and in a different spot from where the original stairs were thought to be located, it seems odd that spectres pre-dating its construction should be seen there (348). But as we have already observed, a similar situation may exist with spectres from the medieval era appearing in the Tudor room built centuries later.

The main staircase also featured in a strange incident that occurred in 1974. Andrew Green writes that resident caretakers, Mr and Mrs Lett, heard the mysterious ringing of bells one evening as they were walking up the main staircase. Mrs Lett remarked that she was puzzled, as there were only two bells at the priory, and neither was ringing at the time. One of the bells, in fact, was tied up to prevent it from sounding, and on that sultry night, there was no wind stirring that could have caused the other bell to move (*Ghosts of the South East*, 71). It is tempting to wonder, however, whether what the Letts heard might not have been the psychic echo of one of the church bells sold from Michelham Priory during the Dissolution of the Monasteries.

In November 1980, Andrew Gottlieb, director of the priory from 1980-1992 and a member of the priory's management committee from 1969, also had an experience he couldn't explain. John Rackham writes that on this late afternoon, the property was closed to the public for the winter, and the staff had already left for the day. The regular caretaker was on holiday, and as the day was blustery, Mr Gottlieb went to check the great barn doors to make sure that they were properly secured. As he passed the front of the priory, he heard a dull thudding sound above his head. When he looked up, he was startled to see a window opening with no sign of a hand pushing it.

This sight was odd enough, as Mr Gottlieb was certain that the priory was locked and unoccupied at the time. The window belonged to a locked storeroom in which items from the property's reserve collection were held. To gain entry, staff members had to go through two more locked doors leading to the storeroom door, and the keys for all three doors were kept in a safe. To Mr Gottlieb's knowledge, no one had entered this room for at least two months.

Still puzzled, he went on to make sure that the barn doors were secure. On his return, he flashed his torch at the storeroom window, finding it still open. When Mr Gottlieb went back inside the priory, the chairman of the Management Committee and his family arrived. When Mr Gottlieb told them about the window opening, the chairman decided to accompany him to the storeroom, where they found all the doors still locked, with no sign that anyone had interfered with them. Mr Gottlieb then went to the open window and found it to be extremely stiff and difficult to move without some exertion. But perhaps the best evidence of all that no living being had opened the window was that upon the dusty floor, there was no evidence whatsoever of footprints.

John Rackham writes that Mr Gottlieb had a second, perhaps even more disturbing experience at Michelham Priory twelve years later. In 1992, some eighty executives, actors, and film crew descended on the property to film an episode in a television drama series, *All the World's A Stage*. A section of the priory's undercroft was set aside for use as a dressing room for male actors, while the rest was utilised as a wig and make-up room. Before the film crew left every evening around 7 PM, a technician washed the seven or eight wigs used by the actors and positioned them on small pedestals to dry overnight. The pedestals themselves were left on chairs.

On the morning of the third day of filming, the woman in charge of the wigs came to complain to Mr Gottlieb. She explained that every morning at 6.45, when the crew had arrived to comb out the wigs and make up the actors, they had found a number of the hairpieces scattered across the floor. Was it possible, she wondered, whether any children living at the priory might have been responsible?

Mr Gottlieb replied that there were no such children, and that even if there had been, the undercroft was locked securely each night and an alarm system was turned on. He assured the technician that he would personally see to the security of the wigs that evening. But even after making sure that the area had been locked and the alarm had been set, Mr Gottlieb still received a shock the next morning. Arriving before the film crew to unlock the doors, he was astounded to see four wigs lying dishevelled upon the floor. According to Rackham, the wigs continued to be disturbed in such a way until the filming ended (348-49).

Andrew Green in *Haunted Sussex Today* writes of a similar incident in which a member of staff as well as two members of a BBC film crew were startled to see a wig that had been carefully hung on the back of a chair 'suddenly leap off and fly across the room'. Shortly after the crew left, Green writes, the manager went upstairs to find the window of a storeroom opening by itself. The manager claimed that the window had probably not been opened for decades, as it was rusted solid. He was able to close and fasten it again only with difficulty (Seaford, East Sussex: S.B. Publications, 1997, 79).

Green says that the incidents described above took place in 1990, but they are remarkably similar to those alleged to have occurred in 1980 and 1992, respectively, as detailed by John Rackham in *Brighton Ghosts, Hove Hauntings*. Again, readers might well ask whether these are truly separate occurrences, or if witnesses or chroniclers have perhaps got their dates or details confused. Such confusion is almost inevitable when tales of the supernatural are told and retold, when details from new stories overlay or become intertwined with aspects of older ones.

What is evident is that the number of paranormal incidents at Michelham Priory seems to have increased during the last two decades. Rackham, for example, writes that on several occasions since 1992, cleaners were perplexed to find that the bedclothes and mattresses on two cots in the children's nursery had been tossed onto the floor. And at the end of October 1993, members of the Ghost Research Foundation based in Surrey were startled by their findings during a night-long Halloween vigil. They locked all the doors of the undercroft and then, to make them doubly secure, sealed them with wire. The four members of the group then put a light dusting of flour on the furniture in the room. Certain that they had been the only ones on the premises, next morning they were delighted to discover a ten-inch-long, skeletal-looking handprint in the dusting of flour on the sideboard. As an added bonus, as two of them were on their way home, they happened to pass the area of the cloister where for about five seconds, they clearly heard what sounded like the chanting of plainsong.

Fred Overty, property manager at the time, told Rackham that in his five years at the priory, he had heard many unexplained crashes and bangs in the night, and he recalled also the strange period in 1995 when a variety of tools used by gardeners and other staff kept disappearing, only to reappear later in different locations. That was the same year, Rackham writes, when a summer visitor claimed to sense an angry presence in a corner of the prior's chamber, in the same locale where others had also reported seeing a shadowy figure (*Brighton Ghosts, Hove Hauntings*, 349-50).

In recent years, in fact, the prior's chamber has been the scene of many odd occurrences. Psychic Kathy Gearing told me that on Halloween 2004, five of her Ghost Club members had a particularly unforgettable experience there. 'They saw a man in a long black coat or cloak, walking fast through the exhibition rooms,' she said. 'Two members were standing on the stairs when they saw him, and followed him into the prior's chamber, where three more members caught a glimpse of him. At first, everyone thought he was a real person, but then he just vanished.'

Kathy's group had experienced an earlier sighting of the same phantom during an investigation held in April 2003. 'We had a very strong sceptic in the group, and he was having problems with the camcorder,' she recalled. 'Every time he went into the dining room, the camcorder just wouldn't work, but when he came out again, it would be fine. He was getting very frustrated and annoyed, until at one point, he came running out to me, white as a sheet. He asked me whether anything had been seen in the music room.'

'"You know that's not how investigations work," I told him. "What have you seen?" As there was no one in the undercroft, we went in there, where he told me about the figure of a man he had seen. He hadn't had the chance to tell anyone else yet, but just as we were leaving, another one of the members came running in, also very excited. He'd seen the same man, in roughly the same place, a few minutes later. Both men had clearly witnessed this apparition wearing a black habit, standing a few feet in front of the end wall of the music room.'

Later that evening, outside in the grounds, the second man saw a group of black-clad canons walking slowly in single file and then disappearing. Kathy, who was with him at the time, saw no apparitions but noticed instead a dull, bluish, mist-like light moving away from the priory.

The most startling result of that April 2003 investigation was yet to come, however. When Kathy and several other members of the group heard unidentifiable sounds of rushing water inside the prior's chamber, they assumed that the radiator was leaking and alerted the property manager. The group also discovered a trace of an oily substance on the windowsill, but found nothing to account for the water sounds. By now the security alarm had been turned off, so the group was able to enter areas normally protected by the alarm to take photographs. They left a camcorder running and took still pictures with their own cameras. Kathy herself snapped a few shots with a digital camera, but it was not until reaching home a few hours later that she finally examined them.

One of the photos clearly shows the figure of a man, standing and facing straight ahead, apparently staring into the lens of the camera. 'We had had a lot of problems with cameras in the prior's chamber,' Kathy explained, 'and this photo seems to have been taken in available light conditions, without my flash going off. The man appears to be wearing either a long coat or cloak, and he seems to have shoulder-length hair and possibly a beard and moustache. I was positive that there was nobody standing in front of me at the time, and the figure does not resemble anyone who was there.'

Kathy recalled also that someone else took a photo of the same spot later in the evening, before anyone had seen her photo. In that second image a 'large, strange yellowy light' appeared where the man had appeared in Kathy's.

Intrigued, she sent copies of the photo she had taken to Ghost Club members who had been present and to photographic analyst Philip Carr, who enhanced the image for more expert examination.

'As I interpret the image,' he wrote back to her, the figure 'appears dressed in dark clothes, heavily bearded and bare-headed with hair reaching down to the shoulders which curls into the neck. The nose and eye sockets are clearly defined. The lighting is ambient, available artificial light. Obviously the flash did not go off or at least synch with the camera, hence the orange light and oblique shadows. So this was no doubt a time exposure. A very interesting picture.' (To see the photo and to read more details of The Ghost Club's investigations at Michelham Priory, visit the organisation's website at http://www.ghostclub.org.uk.)

Another unusual incident involving the group occurred when Kathy Gearing and some other members were inside the music room, which houses a collection of instruments. 'It had been very atmospheric throughout the night,' Kathy told me, 'but by then it had gone really quiet. I said, "If there's anybody here, perhaps you can give us a sign by playing a few notes on one of the instruments." All remained quiet, or so it seemed, but when I spoke to other members of the group that had been elsewhere in the building, they claimed to have heard a short burst of music. One person even managed to record it on his video camera. On the tape, you can hear the members saying to each other, "Can you hear that?" The musical burst, possibly coming from a harpsichord, sounds very old-fashioned and lasts about twenty-five seconds.' Kathy pointed out that the acoustics in the priory make it difficult sometimes to tell where sounds are coming from, but she insisted that there was only one harpsichord on the property.

Her group also witnessed a strange visual phenomenon in the music room. 'I had the entire team of nine people in a circle,' Kathy recalled, 'many of them using dowsing rods. The rods had begun to move quite wildly when about half of the group saw a very bright light appear at the top righthand corner of a tapestry. The light circled over the tapestry and moved very fast toward the middle, stopped for a second and then darted off, disappearing through the wall. Similar lights have been seen prior to or just after the appearance of an apparition.'

One of those apparitions, that of a young girl, has been sighted by several staff members. 'They call her Rosemary,' Kathy Gearing said, 'and while I can't find anything to document her name, several mediums have come up instead with the name Sarah. She's been seen running up and down the stairs quite often, and in early 2004 she was said to be playing with some young lads who were there.'

Kathy had her own run-in with this mischievous phantom at about the same time. 'My mum had gone to investigate the priory with me, and the next morning about six o'clock, after everyone else had gone home, she and I were sitting there in the undercroft,' she recalled. 'We were waiting for the property manager to come along so we could tell him we were leaving. But just then we heard light footsteps coming down the stairs, running through the corridor. We heard the voice of a little girl, laughing her head off; then she ran back again. We both got up and ran to the corridor, but there was no one there.'

'As is the case with so many of these happenings, this seemed absolutely real at the time,' Kathy insisted, 'and not frightening at all. It's only afterwards that you realise that something very strange has occurred. But so much happens there - the priory is definitely one of the most haunted buildings in Sussex. I've not been there for even a single night when something unusual hasn't happened. There are frequent massive drops in temperature, hugely elevated electromagnetic readings, and a feeling of being touched.'

And then there are those unaccountable smells reported frequently by staff and visitors alike. 'Time after time a sudden strong perfume or incense has been noticed on the first floor landing,' Kathy said. 'It suddenly seems to waft up and is smelled by everyone in the vicinity, only to disappear just as quickly. I have checked for the presence of flowers, air fresheners, furniture polishes - all that sort of thing, but they have not been responsible for the aroma. One of the strangest odours was the sudden and intense smell of beef and onions on the top floor. That lasted for about thirty seconds before disappearing, but it was extremely strong.'

Another, much less pleasant smell reported in the undercroft is that of burning hair, experienced both by guides and visitors. Gil Saunders in an article for *Sussex Life* interviewed property manager Fred Overty, who claimed that the stench was at times so intense that he had been forced to leave the undercroft door open (http://www.sussexlife.com/gils_guide/upper_dicker.html).

Phantom sounds as well as smells haunt the priory. 'We've heard what I call "tuneful whistling" on many occasions,' Kathy Gearing continued. 'Again, it doesn't sound at all out of place. You just assume it really is somebody whistling, until you discover differently!'

The first time Kathy experienced this phenomenon, she was with a colleague with whom she was doing some filming. The colleague had just nipped out when Kathy first noticed the whistling. Assuming that the sound was coming from her colleague, Kathy stopped the filming and waited for his return. Eventually, the filming resumed over the old tape that had recorded the whistling, and it was only later that the crew realised, to their dismay, that the sound they had recorded over must have been of paranormal origin.

Kathy recalled that in 2003, during a charity drive by Southern FM Radio, six women took a dictaphone to the gatehouse to do some recording. When their tape was played later, Kathy said, 'you could hear the women clearly in the background, but there is also what appears to be a man's voice begging for help. That's been played on the radio and is quite impressive.'

Unseen horses have also been heard clopping through the gateway of the gatehouse, and human footsteps have been reported echoing along the top floor when no one was there. And according to John Rackham, a young girl and her grandmother had an experience at the gatehouse in the early 1990s that neither is likely to forget.

The grandmother was responsible for a small on-site bakery at the priory, and one day she brought her ten-year-old granddaughter along. They were leaving for home when the young girl asked to go inside the gatehouse. Excited, she ran on ahead and scurried up the staircase, only to return a moment later, pale and upset. From the safety of her grandmother's arms, the girl confessed that she had seen the eerie sight of a fragment of a woman's dress moving by itself down the staircase.

The child's obvious distress, along with the fact that the apparition she described was so out of the ordinary, both indicate that she was telling the truth. As the pair hurried away from the gatehouse, Rackham writes, the grandmother glanced back to see a strange blue glow filling the window on the first floor (350-51).

Other youngsters, along with their teacher, also experienced unusual phenomena on a visit to Michelham Priory. In an entry posted in June 2004 to the Children of the City (COTC) Paranormal Investigations online noticeboard, the teacher at the secondary school near Lewes claims that the students reported a variety of occurrences. These included unexplained cold spots at the foot of the stairs and in the prior's chamber; stones being dropped by no apparent source onto the centre of the floor in one of the upper rooms (also witnessed by the teacher); a distinct sneezing sound from the empty nursery, where another student heard the names Mary, Elizabeth and Rosemary spoken; a student being tapped on the shoulder by an invisible source in the barn; and sudden feelings of nausea arising when students entered the top room at the gatehouse and disappearing when they left.

Most surprising were the results of a dictaphone recording made by the teacher during a tour of the upper floors. On playing back the cassette immediately afterwards, the listeners were startled to hear three shouts of what sounded like either 'No' or 'Whoa' recorded in the prior's chamber, as well as five screams, sounding like those of a young girl, recorded in the music room adjoining the nursery. The children were all remarkably well-behaved during the visit, the teacher insists, a fact that was confirmed by the tour guide and other staff members, so the sounds could not be attributed to unruly pupils. The teacher goes on to say that staff members who listened to the recordings were visibly shaken, and requested a copy of the tape to add to their archives. Another copy was offered to the COTC group (see the teacher's posting and the follow-up response by the COTC at http://cotcpi.proboards23.com/index.cgi?board=general&action=print&board=general&num=1087986853).

The COTC itself has conducted several investigations of the priory, the first in early November 2002 (read their reports at http://www.cotcpi.co.uk and http://www.freewebs.com/almosthaunted/michelhampriory.htm#23907841).
During the first investigation, the group held several séances that revealed the presence of a frightened, abused child named Rosie and an older female, Jennifer, who said she felt helpless to protect Rosie from being hurt by an unidentified man. Group leader Stacey Logan also claimed to make contact with a spirit called Robert Henry Sackville who told the group that they were not welcome. This spirit named a Mary and a Jennifer as members of his family, and added that his sons were 'murderous traitors'. He then gave the group members a formal warning to leave.

Undaunted, the COTC returned twice to Michelham Priory in 2004, once on 25 May and again on Halloween. During the May visit, the group photographed several orbs and a cloaked figure in the garden. The resulting image of this apparition shows only what looks like blue smoke or flame. Group members also sensed the presence of several entities, including a man called Jonathan, a man who told the group to leave, a man chasing the girl called Rosie who runs away from him, a crying woman, and, again, the older female spirit called Jennifer who repeats her regret at not being able to protect Rosie from abuse. COTC members then held a séance at which the irritable male spirit again told them to get out of 'his' house.

When the group returned several months later for their Halloween visit, they were reportedly plagued by unusual feelings of unease, as if they were being watched and followed. Some members also reported a strange feeling that the stairs were dangerous, even sensing the presence of a man called Jacob who had fallen to his death there. They sensed also the presence of a woman named Hanna who had tended Jacob as he lay dying, and of a former gardener. Interestingly, as a guest at one of The Ghost Club investigations in 2003, COTC leader Stacey Logan had sensed that another person, this time a woman named

Mary Howell, perhaps a maid or lady in waiting, had also fallen down the stairs or over the banisters.

During their Halloween 2004 investigation, COTC members took photographs of orbs, felt cold spots, smelled incense in the music room, and heard mysterious thudding sounds on grass. Group members also reported hearing footsteps on gravel behind the hedgerows, an especially perplexing development since this area is covered by grass only, with no gravel at all. The investigators also witnessed cradles in the 'children's bedroom', presumably the nursery, rocking by themselves, and wound up with a séance in the music room, during which they claimed to contact the spirit of a man called Thomas who told them rudely and repeatedly to leave 'his' house. This spirit was identified wrongly at first as previous owner Thomas Sackville, who bought the priory in 1601. Later the spirit was believed instead to be that of Thomas Cromwell, who received the property from Henry VIII in 1537 but was later executed by him just three years later.

Visitors to Michelham Priory will have no difficulty in understanding why the spirits of Thomas Cromwell and the others might be so loath to leave their former home. Even those entities who might have experienced suffering during their time there surely cannot help but be amazed, reassured, and comforted by the peaceful, beautiful property it has now become.

ℵewhaven Fort

NEWHAVEN, EAST SUSSEX

It's hard to get people to agree on just who or what is haunting Newhaven Fort, but nearly everyone connected with this Victorian installation admits that there are some strange goings-on there. Built by Lord Palmerston in the 1860s to protect against French invasion, the fort also saw use in both the First and Second World Wars, before falling into disrepair when the army finally left in 1956. In 1981 Lewes District Council took over the facility, and the next year the restored Newhaven Fort was opened to the public as a museum.

Most reports of the supernatural at the fort centre on the passageways, especially the caponier, a tunnel that goes down to the beach. Here staff members and visitors alike have reported feeling a presence, with some experiencing even more physical manifestations.

'Close to Halloween in about 1996 I was going down to check the lights in the tunnel,' one staff member told me. 'It's very damp down there, and claustrophobic. I had the feeling that my shoulders were being crushed as I tried to walk through the little passageway. It was just like I was being pushed back. It was hard to walk through the tunnel, and on the way back, I was sort of shoved out. I've been down there loads of time since then, but I've never felt that since.'

'We've had a number of questions from visitors about whether there's a ghost down there,' she continued. 'And people who used to work here years ago said things had happened to them, but it was so long ago we don't remember what they said anymore!'

In the late nineteenth century, about a hundred soldiers would have been stationed at Newhaven Fort, and the echoing sounds of their boots are said still to be heard marching through the corridors, barrack rooms and tunnels. Air raid sirens from a more recent era have also reportedly been heard, according to R. Stevens-Bassett in his *Ghostly Tales & Hauntings of East Sussex* (CLX, 1993, 48).

A group of paranormal investigators known as the Children of the City (COTC) visited Newhaven Fort in October 2002 and wrote up their findings on their website at http://www.cotcpi.co.uk/newhaven%20fort%20report.htm. Stacey Logan, co-director and clairvoyant of the group, interviewed staff members about their experiences and decided to hold several séances, during which the investigators felt the presence of a man whose name was later spelt out on a Ouija board as Robert James.

The séances revealed that James worked at the fort and was killed there as the result of a fall in 1935, when he was forty-three years old. James was trapped, probably by an explosion, and he wanted the group to help him find a way out. According to the investigators, the spirit said that a nearby tunnel was blocked and that he was forbidden to pass through a door marked 'for officers only'. The other end of the tunnel was black. The investigators told the spirit to light a lamp in order to find his way out, which he apparently did. During the filming of the séance, a sound like a horn being blown was recorded.

In another séance, the COTC investigators claimed to contact a spirit called Peter, who claimed to be a 'domestic' who was 'watching for the French'. This spirit also told the group that people laughed at him because of the appearance of his face. The investigators believed that he had suffered either from burns or leprosy.

Philip Baldock, a technical assistant at Newhaven Fort, had heard other stories about the identity of the phantom presence. 'There was a royal artillery gunner named Beard who was killed about the time the fort was built, when they were moving the guns in,' he told me. 'I don't know exactly what happened, but he was crushed, I assume. He was buried with military honours.'

Still others believe that the passageways at Newhaven Fort are haunted by the ghost of Edward Cooke, a soldier who was executed for his part in the so-called East Blatchington Mutiny of 1795. Cooke was a member of the Oxfordshire Militia billeted in Seaford. Living conditions were terrible, and the soldiers were not given proper rations but forced to buy overpriced food of bad quality. In protest one day, Cooke and some other soldiers raided a butcher's shop and paraded through town with joints of meat stuck onto their bayonets.

The next day they hijacked a boat laden with flour meant for export and immediately sold the flour at cheap prices to equally hungry members of the public.

Six of the men were caught and marched to Brighton for court-martial. The townsfolk of Brighton sympathised with the soldiers and crowded the streets to offer them food and encouragement. Edward Cooke and Sam Parrish, considered to be the ringleaders, said in their defence statements that the flour they had seized was being exported abroad when they and their families were starving. Even though the people of Brighton petitioned for clemency, Cooke and Parrish were condemned to death, and the four others were sentenced to three hundred lashes, later reduced to one hundred and fifty.

On 13 June 1795, all of the Oxfordshire Militia was ordered to watch the men being lashed. Then Edward Cooke and Sam Parrish were made to kneel beside waiting coffins while ten of their companions were forced, as part of their own punishment, to execute them. After the firing squad's first round, Cooke was still alive, so an officer shot him once more. The remaining soldiers were then marched past the open coffins holding the bodies of the executed men. Later, it was said that these same poorly made coffins oozed blood onto the shoulders of those who carried the executed men to their graves.

The day before his execution, Edward Cooke had written a letter to his brother, saying 'I am going to die for what the regiment done. I am not afraid to meet death for I have done no harm to no person and that is a great comfort to me'.

The unidentified author of a website article describing the mutiny claims not to know why Cooke's ghost is believed to haunt Newhaven Fort, but he relates an incident that occurred when he told the soldier's story in the Grand Magazine ammunition store there.

'Two candles burned in the darkness behind me,' he writes, 'and when I told of the letter to his brother and the execution these candles hissed, guttered and died right down, nearly going out.' The author insists that there was no wind or other air disturbance at the time, and that the other people present felt shivers down their spines (http://www.lhi.org.uk/docs/Tidemillsstories.doc).

Perhaps R. Stevens-Bassett's tale of a ghostly lone Drummer Boy also originates from the East Blatchington Mutiny. Stevens-Bassett gives few details, saying only that according to popular belief, the Drummer Boy haunting the coastline from Newhaven Fort along Seaford Bay was 'hanged for his part in a mutiny on board ship during the eighteenth century' (*Ghostly Tales and Hauntings of East Sussex*, CLX, 1993, 48). Notice that in this version, however, the sailor was executed by hanging rather than by being lashed or shot.

It is perhaps surprising that no one has advanced another possibility for the identity of at least one of the ghosts at Newhaven Fort. In November 1974, when Lord Lucan disappeared from his home in London, a car he had been driving was found abandoned in Newhaven. Thinking that he might have been hiding out in the tunnels, police made a search of the fort to no avail. Lord Lucan has never been found, dead or alive, but his story, too, has now become interwoven with all the others at this historic spot on the Sussex coastline.

Regardless of who or what is responsible for the hauntings there, any site where so much has occurred is bound to possess echoes from the past. Visitors looking for a psychic glimpse into earlier times just may find it at Newhaven Fort.

Nymans Garden
HANDCROSS, NEAR HAYWARDS HEATH, WEST SUSSEX

The ghost of a notorious highwayman is said to be lurking still in the vicinity of Nymans Garden, a glorious property developed by three generations of the Messel family and now owned by the National Trust. With its historic collection of flowers, shrubs and trees from all over the world, not to mention the ruins of a picturesque manor house with several restored rooms to wander in, Nymans Garden is a relaxing and beautiful place to unwind from the stress of daily life.

But visitors might be wise to keep on the lookout for the spectre of Jack Reeding (or Reding, as the name is sometimes spelled), a ruthless robber who used to hide out in a cave in the nearby Nymans Woods. When he was eventually apprehended for his crimes, Jack was hanged outside The Red Lion public house in the adjoining village of Handcross.

But old rogues often turn into something like heroes with the passage of time. An area of Nymans Wood was christened Reedings Wood in Jack's honour, and a Highwayman's Trail for children further commemorates the thief in Nymans Garden.

Leonard Messel, who bequeathed the property to the National Trust in 1953, wrote a letter believed to be still in the Nymans archives, claiming to have seen Jack's ghost one evening while he was fishing. Messel apparently witnessed the apparition of the highwayman charging through the woods on his horse, and the story is that Jack may be seen riding through the woods to this day.

Pallant House Gallery

CHICHESTER, WEST SUSSEX

It will be interesting to find out whether Pallant House, newly refurbished and reopened as a gallery for modern art in the South, has managed to retain its ghosts. But judging by the number of uncanny experiences related to me by former members of staff, it's a good bet that at least some of the supernatural tenants of the Queen Anne-era building will have decided to remain.

Pallant House, in the heart of Chichester, has long been recognised by architectural historians as one of the most important eighteenth-century town houses in the country. Built in 1712-13 by young wine merchant Henry Peckham and his wife Elizabeth, the house was considered to be the last word in modernity. Its elegant, restrained features must have looked completely out of place in this industrial part of town, where the surrounding buildings were mainly tanneries, brewhouses, and malthouses. Pallant House itself was constructed on the foundations of an old malthouse, and was modelled from a particular style of London house chosen by the Peckhams to impress their neighbours. Their marriage wasn't happy, and the couple split up after only a few years. A succession of private owners then occupied Pallant House in the eighteenth and nineteenth centuries, and in 1919 it was purchased by the Westhampnett Rural District Council, before being restored and turned into an art gallery for the first time in 1982.

In March 1998, I spoke with several former staff members of Pallant House about the strange goings-on there. The most often reported occurrence seemed to be unexplained cooking smells emanating from what was known as the Victorian kitchen. Nigel Draycott, the former Education Officer of Pallant House, explained that the original kitchen had been built at the back of the house, but that in the nineteenth century, a new kitchen had been put into the main building.

'So we know that the ghost causing the smells is somebody who was in the house from that date onwards,' Nigel told me. 'A lot of people have actually smelled cooking from the Victorian kitchen as they go up the back staircase. A friend of mine says that she has smelled a very sweet smell, as if someone is baking something. I know of at least three people who have had this experience, independent of each other.'

Staff members Sybil Grindrod and Angela Clatterback agreed that many people have experienced the odour of bread and cakes wafting through the air, and Angela herself had detected 'really sweet, sickly smells' when walking through the kitchen. But other unexplained sensations have been more disturbing.

'Once a party of our friends came round,' Sybil recalled, 'and I asked one of them who was psychic whether she sensed anything. "Yes, come with me," she said, and as she stood by the doorway into the room where the Bow porcelain collection was kept, she said that she felt a presence. She also felt cold. The only place where I have felt anything unusual is in the corner of the kitchen, by the fireplace. It's just sort of an unexplained cold feeling.'

Sybil pointed out that the Peckhams during their short married life had had many quarrels, and that perhaps their constant warring had created something of an unhappy atmosphere in the house.

Angela went on to tell me about another odd experience she had had. 'The administrator and I were here one night when there was a function down in the main gallery,' she said. 'We were in the Victorian kitchen, and the bar was ready and waiting for people to finish, as it was quite late and dark. Suddenly one of the kitchen chairs moved. It was as if someone had been sitting there and then got up, scraping against the flagstone floor. Nobody was near the chair, but it scraped against the floor just as if someone's weight had just moved off it. It was the strangest thing. The hair on the back of my neck just stood up.'

I was told that one woman who had worked at Pallant House in various capacities and over a period of time had actually seen the ghost several times, but claimed not to be frightened of it. 'When the house was used for district council offices,' Nigel Draycott told me, 'one of the staff working for the council came in one day and was very frightened, but this other lady wasn't, as she has always felt that the ghost is benevolent. She suspects that the figure she has seen is a housemaid, because she has a big bunch of keys on her waistband. She wears her hair with a central parting and a bun at the back of her head, but the lady has never seen her face. The ghost appears most often on the half-landing on the big staircase, underneath the big window.

'This woman has also sensed the presence of the ghost even when she doesn't actually see her,' Nigel continued. 'Once at Christmastime we opened up the house and had lots of children here, so the place had a very friendly, almost family-like feeling about it. The woman said, "The ghost is here and very happy that the house has such a happy atmosphere."'

We can only hope that Pallant House will also retain that happy atmosphere in its new function as a modern art gallery for the people of southern England, and that its ghosts, likewise, will remain.

Photo courtesy of Rosemary Appleton.

Pashley Manor Gardens
TICEHURST, NEAR WADHURST, EAST SUSSEX

Visitors to Pashley Manor Gardens are not allowed inside the timber-framed house, unfortunately. But as they wander amongst the roses, ponds, and ancient oaks in this quintessentially English setting, they might give a thought to the ghosts who have also made the place their home.

It's not surprising that such an old property should have a few otherworldly inhabitants. Pashley Manor dates back to 1292, when the de Passele family built a manor with a moat (the moat still exists), owning it until 1453 when the Bullens (or Boleyns) from Norfolk bought it. The most famous member of that family, Anne Boleyn, is believed to have stayed at Pashley Manor during her childhood. The property stayed with the Boleyns until 1543, when it was purchased by Sir Thomas May. Sir Thomas constructed the present Tudor-framed house in 1550, and another member of the May family added a Georgian façade in 1720.

A series of owners have lived at Pashley Manor since then, but perhaps the strangest tale from its history concerns the original inhabitants, the de Passeles. In March 1327, Sir Edmund de Passele and his son William both died suddenly under mysterious circumstances. At this time, another son, Robert, became the heir. Before his death, Edmund had appointed his wife Margaret to be chief executor of his will, but proceedings were delayed because it was never clear that

Margaret and Edmund had been legally married. On the death of his first wife, Maud, Edmund had married a woman named Joan, who then petitioned King Edward III to protest that Margaret had been living with Edmund 'impurely'.

Thus caught out, Edmund was told to return to Joan, and Margaret, fearing the loss of Pashley Manor, decided to poison both Edmund and his eldest son, William, the child of deceased wife Maud. To secure her position even further, Margaret went on to kill thirteen-year-old Edmund, son of Joan, as well as the boy's valet, John Walet. In spite of years of legal wrangling and Margaret's surrendering to the authorities only to escape again, the villainous woman was never punished for her crimes.

No one has been able to identify any of the ghosts at Pashley Manor for certain, but perhaps one of them at least might have some connection with this long-ago murder. Andrew Green in his *Ghosts of the South East* describes an eerie experience late one afternoon by a 'sensitive' observer who saw the figure of a woman standing on the island in the pond known as 'the moat'. The apparition looked down into the water, and after a few seconds she faded away. But the unusual thing about this sighting was that behind the ghostly woman herself, another kind of 'phantom' was seen, what the observer described as the outline of a 'really old building' that no longer exists ('Pashley Manor, Ticehurst,' Newton Abbot: David & Charles, 1976, 103-11).

This occurrence took place during the tenure of the Forsyth family, who owned Pashley Manor from just after the Second World War until 1960. When the Forsyths' daughter Lindsay was nine years old, she often saw the property's best known ghost, an old lady wearing a grey dress who appeared to walk through a partition wall from one bedroom to another. When her father wanted to brick up a fireplace in the wall, Lindsay protested, saying, 'The old lady won't be able to visit me now'.

The Cole family were the next to own Pashley Manor, and Mrs Cole's grandmother was a descendant of the May family who had lived at the house centuries earlier. When the Coles removed some old plaster from the wall facing the stairs, they revealed the framework of a Tudor doorway. Only then, Andrew Green explained, did they understand the tales they had heard from previous residents about the little old lady walking through the wall. She had actually been walking through the original front door!

This phantom, usually described as wearing nineteenth-century clothing, is clearly not the same as the apparition sighted near the pond, who dates from a much earlier era. In addition to walking through walls, this spectre from the Victorian period was also observed on the terrace 'gliding toward one of the pools', according to Green. Nearly everyone who has encountered her has described her as harmless, even charming, and Mrs Cole explained to Green that although she never saw the lady in grey, she often sensed a 'benign presence' in the hallway.

Soldiers living in the house during the Second World War were startled by the appearance of this same ghost on at least one occasion, and earlier than that, around 1918, servants at Pashley Manor claimed to have several run-ins with the lady in grey and other strange phenomena.

Andrew Green reported that practically every member of the staff had seen the apparition, and he interviewed a woman named Madge who vividly recalled her own encounter with the lady. In her teens Madge was an under parlour maid at Pashley, and one day she was in a bedroom collecting boots that needed to be cleaned after a shooting party. When she looked up towards the open door, she saw the gliding figure of a woman, moving along the front landing and swinging her arms, as if she were walking purposefully on some kind of errand.

Madge described the apparition as having 'white hair piled on her head rather like a bun' and wearing 'a high-necked shirt blouse, shaped and gathered into a very small waist'. As the figure had just turned to come up the stairs, Madge was unable to see her face, but she noticed an 'air of grace and charm' about the lady. Oddly, Madge saw only the top half of the woman, as she 'just faded into nothingness at the waist'. Unafraid but intensely curious, Madge followed the phantom into the Violet Room, only to find that she had vanished.

Other members of staff had seen the figure in the Oak Room just opposite, and once, after a ball, a gown that had been hung on a wardrobe to air was knocked unaccountably to the floor by an unseen entity. Even more dramatic, Green writes that in the same area of the house, several members of staff were awakened early one morning by the sounds of rattling china and knocking on two bedroom doors. Eeriest of all was the report of a cook, who 'on a winter's evening' claimed to have witnessed 'phantom hands grasping out through the balustrades at the top of the stairs'.

Besides the two phantom ladies, the disembodied hands, and the assorted poltergeist-like activities reported at Pashley Manor, there is also the mysterious figure seen by Mrs Cole. One night Rufus, one of her eight children, was lying ill in the small room next to hers, his door kept slightly open by a sausage-shaped draft excluder on the floor. A light was on in the corridor, and Mrs Cole's bedroom door was open.

Suddenly Mrs Cole awoke to the sight of a small figure standing in the doorway, about four and a half feet tall and wearing what seemed to be a dressing gown. Believing that it was Rufus, she called out to him. Without answering, the figure moved away, and Mrs Cole hurried into Rufus' room. There all trace of the figure was gone, and her son was found to be in a high fever, lying in a spread-eagle position on the bed.

As Mrs Cole had had to push the door open further to enter Rufus' room, causing the draft excluder to rattle as she did so, she was certain that her son had never left his bed to come to her, as she had heard no sound before the mysterious figure appeared.

Andrew Green wonders whether this small phantom might also be responsible for the pitiful, unexplained crying sounds that Mrs Cole often heard coming from the direction of the moat. It was usually on a Saturday morning when she was in the old kitchen that she heard the 'creepy' wailing of a child yelling 'Maa…my' echoing through the trees and across the terrace. Green doesn't make the connection, but is it possible that the cries heard by Mrs Cole could have been those of thirteen-year-old Edmund de Passele, murdered in the fourteenth century by the wicked Margaret?

Still other strange occurrences have been reported in a flat occupied by a gardener and his wife at the end of the main building. This area is accessible only by means of an outside stairway, and according to Green, the sound of footsteps has been heard going up the stairs when no one was there.

One evening the eldest son of the family received quite a fright. He was standing at the bottom of the stairs when he heard the footsteps pass right by him as they continued on their way up to the flat. His mother sensed that something evil was connected with the sound but she was unable to say why. Some workmen also claimed to be so frightened by the atmosphere that they refused to be left alone there.

Visitors to Pashley Manor Gardens need have no such worries, however, as they stroll amongst the lush flowers and fountains of this magical place. If they do encounter any of the ghosts that still linger about the grounds, they should just consider these supernatural tenants as yet another feature of this charming historic property.

Pevensey Castle

PEVENSEY, EAST SUSSEX

uilt around 290 A.D., Pevensey Castle has served as a military fortress for more than 1,700 years. Originally called *Anderida*, the stronghold was probably constructed during the usurpation of Britain by two rebellious Romans, Carausius and Allectus, whose images on gold coins have been found in the castle's foundations. In 286 Carausius, commander of a piracy-fighting fleet in the English Channel, was accused of keeping captured booty instead of turning it over to the imperial treasury. In response to the charge, Carausius proclaimed himself emperor, not only of Britain but also of parts of Gaul. His reign was short-lived, however, as former follower Allectus assassinated him and became his successor in 293. It's likely that both usurpers felt the need to build coastal fortifications such as those at Pevensey, not only to protect themselves from raiding Saxons but also from central Roman authority. Indeed, in spite of these defences, Allectus was overthrown by a full-scale Roman invasion after just three years.

For another hundred years or so, until the Romans withdrew from Britain in the early fifth century, *Anderida* provided protection from Saxon pirates. But the *Anglo Saxon Chronicle* records that in 491, a few decades after the Roman departure, raiders led by Aella the Saxon besieged the castle and slaughtered a British community sheltering within its walls. No further mention is made of Pevensey Castle for almost six hundred years, until 28 September 1066, when

William, Duke of Normandy, landed in the nearby bay and began erecting new structures within the castle.

William's conquest of England ushered in an era of refortification, and in 1088 the structure took centre stage in the battle for succession involving William's sons, Duke Robert of Normandy and the ultimately victorious William Rufus. In all, Pevensey Castle was besieged four times but never captured, only twice surrendering because of famine. The ancient fortress was last called into service during the Second World War, when it was used as a command and observation post. Now it is managed by English Heritage.

Such a long and varied history has given Pevensey Castle more than its fair share of supernatural phenomena, much of it of a military nature. Robert A. Stevens, who leads historical walks in Pevensey and Alfriston, and who has written several books about Sussex ghosts, told me about the phantom Roman army that has been heard marching near the castle.

'Quite a few people have told me that they've heard voices and the sound of feet marching past, although the streets were empty at the time,' Robert said. 'The old Roman road ran through the village, through the castle, and out through Westham. The sounds have been heard along that route.'

Unexplained noises of battle have also been reported at night from inside the castle walls. Andrew Green writes that in August 1970 he was told of several people who had heard the sounds, and who associated them with the landing of William in 1066 (Sussex Pamphlets, Napier Publications, 21). Still other people in the Pevensey area have reported hearing the moans of dying and injured soldiers drifting over from the site of the Battle of Hastings, especially around the time of its anniversary, on the 14th of October.

Phantom troops have been seen as well as heard, proceeding at night across the marshes to Pevensey Castle. Peter Underwood in *The A-Z of British Ghosts* writes that armour and weapons have been observed glinting in the moonlight, although in this case, 'no sound is heard, as the ghostly army, led by William Rufus, who once fruitlessly attacked the old castle for six days, silently disappears into the moat' (London: Chancellor Press, 1992, 185).

Marc Alexander in *Haunted Castles* writes that if there are ghosts at Pevensey Castle, surely they would be of the Britons who were slaughtered there during the raid of Aella the Saxon (London: Frederick Muller, 1974, 35). The ruthless fifth-century king is indeed believed to have slain every man, woman, and child he found within the castle walls, yet I was unable to find even a single account involving the spirits of the murdered Britons. What I did find, however, was the tale of the phantom Drummer Boy who tried to warn them about the impending attack.

'That's quite a well-known story,' Robert Stevens told me. 'The ghostly Drummer Boy is always heard but never seen, in both the village of Pevensey and the castle, but not on the Westham side. Someone was supposed to have heard him in 2003, up by the drawbridge to the Norman castle. Newhaven Fort and Herstmonceux Castle also have similar tales - I believe that the ghostly Drummer Boy is an example of an apocryphal story that attaches itself to lots of different places.'

Probably the most famous supernatural story at Pevensey Castle is that of the Pale Lady who is often seen pacing the outer walls, usually at dusk. Most people believe her to be Lady Joan Pelham, whose husband, Sir John, was appointed constable of the castle by the Duke of Lancaster in 1394. Five years later the Duke's son, Henry Bolingbroke, usurped the crown to become Henry IV, leaving Sir John no choice but to support him in his fight against Richard II. Sir John duly headed off to Yorkshire, leaving his wife at home. A large army of Richard's forces besieged the castle, trapping Lady Joan inside. She smuggled a letter to her husband, warning him of the attack, and was somehow able literally to 'hold the fort' until the Duke's army arrived to relieve her. Now, over six hundred years later, a misty shape or the more definite figure of a woman occasionally forms on the castle walls, and many believe it to be the wraith of Lady Joan, anxiously watching out for her husband's return.

Andrew Green writes of a 'Mr Brownlow' who described his sister's sighting in early 1970 of a woman he believed to be Lady Joan, 'dressed in peculiar clothes' and standing on the walls (Sussex Pamphlets, Napier Publications, 21). Later, in *Ghosts of Today,* Green writes that in 1976 a group of four local boys were 'larking about' when they saw 'a female figure gliding on the top of the walls' (London: Kaye & Ward, 1980, 45-46). The boys were so frightened that they 'dared the wrath of the custodian' and reported the sighting to him. Green retells the story in *Haunted Sussex Today* and adds that the custodian was so impressed with the boys' account that he made an official entry of it in his records. The author then goes on to say that the phantom was sighted again one afternoon in September 1984 by a group of twelve young visitors, who were 'puzzled by the appearance of a woman in medieval dress standing at the bottom of Castle Hill'. The visitors were even more dumbstruck, Green writes, when the woman vanished as they approached her (Seaford, East Sussex: S.B. Publications, 1997, 58-59).

R. Stevens-Bassett in his *Ghostly Tales & Hauntings of East Sussex* tells of a similar incident involving a group of teenagers who had pitched their tent near the castle in late summer 1984. As night began to fall, they saw someone walking along the south side of the structure. This figure, he writes, was dressed in a long white coat and for all intents and purposes, appeared to be 'a real person walking a dog'. The only unusual aspect of this sighting was that the figure appeared not to be walking, but 'moving along as if floating'. Intrigued, the teenagers ran after the person, 'clambering over a fence and up the ruins which the ghost had effortlessly glided across'. But as the figure reached a large bush in the shadow of the castle walls, it suddenly vanished. When the teens reached the spot, they found neither a person nor a dog (CLX, 1993, 11).

This account doesn't reveal the sex of the floating figure seen by the teenagers, but in nearly all such reports, the apparition is clearly a woman. Not everyone agrees, however, that the so-called Pale Lady is Joan Pelham. Another contender for the ghost's identity is Queen Joanna of Navarre, whose story, like Lady Joan's, also concerns Henry IV.

In 1399, the same year that Lady Joan defended the castle for the usurping Henry IV, Duchess Joanna of Brittany made up her mind to marry him. Joanna, the mother of nine children, refused to let anything stand in her way, not even the fact that she was already married. Her plan came closer to fulfilment later that year when her elderly husband conveniently died, making it possible for Joanna to marry Henry by proxy in April 1402 and to come to England herself a year later.

By all accounts the couple were very happy together until Henry died just a few years later, in 1413. In 1419 his son, Henry V, accused his stepmother of witchcraft and seized her property. Although never tried, Joanna was imprisoned for three years at Pevensey Castle until her stepson, then on his deathbed, developed a guilty conscience and withdrew all charges. Joanna was finally released and her property and position returned to her, along with enough fine cloth for five or six new gowns, meant to make up for the privations she had suffered in prison. Henry V apparently knew all along that his stepmother was innocent, but he had probably been motivated by greed for her wealth. Queen Joanna's incarceration at Pevensey Castle must have been one of the loneliest and most miserable experiences of her life, so it's hardly surprising that some believe it to be she, rather than Lady Joan Pelham, who haunts the scene of her former despair.

One more ghost, that of a mysterious black monk, is said to glide from time to time through the grounds of the castle and then through the village, all the way to Westham Church. But who he is or why he is there, no one seems to know (R. Stevens-Bassett, 44).

Nor does anyone know who or what was responsible for hurling stones at a group of investigators in the late summer of 1997. Paul Holloway, a member of Sussex Southern Research based in Eastbourne, has been visiting Pevensey Castle with the group for the last ten to twelve years.

'We were there with another paranormal organisation one afternoon,' he told me, 'leaning on the railing above the dungeon, looking out and away from the castle. Suddenly we heard a tapping noise and turned around to see tiny pebbles that looked as if they were being thrown from the top of a wall. They were coming down quite hard, making a distinct noise when they landed.'

'We laughed and joked about it, and one of us yelled, "Pack it in!" We turned around and looked away, and then it all started again,' Paul said. 'We looked to see whether the stones were being blown off, but there wasn't any wind. No one that we could see was throwing them down, but because of the angle they were falling, we could tell that they were being propelled. The pelting lasted for several minutes, but when we shouted again for it to stop, it did.'

Paul's group had another unexplained experience that same day. 'We were walking into the tower near the entrance, the one nearest the English Heritage hut,' he recalled. 'Our group came inside, onto the timber floor, and then we stopped. But the sound of four extra footsteps carried on walking across the floor! There were seven or eight of us there, and we all heard it. And these weren't quick steps, either, but quite measured ones. Four deliberate steps, and they definitely weren't an echo.'

Three years later, in August 2000, Paul was conducting a ghost walk for about thirty people around the grounds of the castle. 'As we walked onto the footbridge, I was talking about the ghosts and what our group had experienced in the past,' Paul explained. 'Suddenly, the strongest smell of lavender appeared out of nowhere. Everybody on the bridge smelled it. It lasted about thirty seconds and then just faded away. There were no lavender bushes anywhere around, but that scent is one of the best known indicators of ghostly activity. Later, one of the men who had been standing on the bridge came up to me. He was normally quite a sceptic, but he said that when the scent of lavender appeared, he had felt an unseen hand touch his shoulder.'

Other strange phenomena have also been reported at the castle. Andrew Green in *Haunted Sussex Today* writes that in 1993 a team of archaeologists based near the south wall were annoyed when the refrigerator in their storage hut wouldn't work. To make repairs, it was necessary to gain access to the main fuse box located in a room in the north-east tower. The archaeologists had to call out a security man from Eastbourne to get to the fuse box, as it was located behind a securely locked iron gate. The incident was really of little importance, Green writes, except that the group was puzzled as to who could have gained access to the fuse box in the first place to cut off the power.

The archaeologists were even more perplexed on two consecutive mornings to discover footprints in the dew-covered grass, leading away from the site of the chapel to the outer south wall where the Pale Lady has often been seen. Oddly, however, there were no footprints leading *toward* the chapel, so how did anyone get to the chapel in the first place without leaving any? Even stranger, Green writes, is the fact that the same phenomena were repeated the next year, at the start of the 1994 digging season (Seaford, East Sussex: S.B. Publications, 1997, 58-60).

In April 2002, the paranormal research group Children Of The City (COTC) conducted a Pevensey Castle investigation and presented the results along with photographs on the organisation website (http://www.cotcpi.co.uk). Members of the group, led by co-founders Stacey and Stuart Logan, set up video cameras in three places - the South Tower, the parapets, and the courtyard. In the early evening hours, a sea mist rolled in, engulfing the grounds. Many of the COTC members reported seeing a group of strangers, all walking toward the castle keep. When the team members tried to follow the mysterious people, however, they found no one there.

The group also turned its attention toward other parts of the castle. The dungeon, said to cause unexplained feelings of nausea in some people, was found to hold 'a very darkened and sinister atmosphere', and photographs taken there showed the presence of mist and orbs, the mysterious balls of light believed by some investigators to be psychic manifestations of energy.

More mist and orbs were found in photographs of the North Tower, which COTC members considered to be the most psychically active room at Pevensey Castle. At one point in the evening, Stacey Logan and another member felt a presence going past them down the stairs into the North Tower room. Stacey reports that when she turned to see what it was, she somehow received a knock on her cheek that left it sore and red. Curiously, however, she writes that after discussing the matter with other members, they attributed the incident more to 'an accident by spirit' than an actual threat.

The group also claimed to hear 'strange thumping noises' coming from below the ground. Were these caused by one of the phantom armies rumoured to haunt the vicinity?

COTC investigators also recorded EVP, or 'electronic voice phenomena' at Pevensey Castle. To accomplish this, group members lowered a microphone into the oubliette, a small prison cell whose only entrance is a hole in the ground. According to the Institute of Paranormal Research website, the voices of two investigators can be heard at the beginning of the playback, followed by an unidentified sound that was not heard during the recording itself. Interested readers may listen for themselves at http://www.iopr.org.uk/4859/?*session*id*key*=*session*id*val*.

Members of DelCo Paranormal Research, an American group headquartered in Delaware County, Pennsylvania, have also visited the castle. Photographs on their website reveal a strange mist at a doorway near the castle's front entrance, as well as an orb on the stairs descending into the North Tower (http://www.delcoghosts.com/pevensey.html and http://www.delcoghosts.com/pevensey2.html). The website writer notes that the photos showing the strange phenomena were taken immediately after her youngest daughter had called out the name of 'Lady Pelham' (http://www.delcoghosts.com/pevenseyhistory.html).

Some might say that there are so many eerie occurrences within the grounds of Pevensey Castle that they have seemingly spilled over into adjacent areas. The Old Mint House, a timber-framed structure immediately outside the castle's east gate, has long been the scene of reputed hauntings, although in this case they all appear to result from an especially grisly double murder.

The Old Mint House, now an antiques shop, was probably built around 1342 on the site of a mint that produced coins during the Norman period. The house was home in the sixteenth century to 'Merry Andrew' Borde, the eccentric scholar, monk and author who served as physician to Henry VIII. Later, in 1586, a London merchant named Thomas Dight was said to have lived in the house with his mistress, a woman identified by Desmond Seward as Eleanor Fitzjohn (*Sussex*, London: Pimlico, 1995, 161).

One evening Dight arrived home unexpectedly, to find Eleanor in the arms of her lover, a handsome young fisherman. Dight and his servants bound up the two young people, then took a sharp knife to cut out Eleanor's tongue. Next they dragged her and the fisherman into the room known as the minting chamber, where they hastily built a fire on the floor. Eleanor was forced to watch helplessly as they suspended her lover in chains from an oak beam in the ceiling. From there he swung in torment, roasting slowly to death.

Accounts vary as to whether Eleanor bled to death or was left to starve in one of the upper rooms. Stories vary also regarding the disposal of the bodies, with some saying that both corpses were buried behind the house. Others say that the fisherman's body was thrown into either the river or the sea, and that Eleanor's was disposed of somewhere inside or near the house. Some versions emphasize that the fisherman was naked when he was strung up to die, and others claim that Eleanor's tongue was cut out after, not before, her lover was killed. But all the versions agree that the crime never would have been discovered if it were not for the deathbed confession of Thomas Dight in 1601.

Robert Stevens agrees that the Old Mint House probably is haunted, but he has doubts about the legend of the double murder. 'I think it was probably invented about fifty years ago,' he told me. 'It's a good story, but it's so bizarre, and the roasting over the fire is a bit much! Some people say that one of the previous owners made it up, and as the place used to be a tea room, maybe they told the tale to add to the atmosphere.'

In spite of his doubts, Robert has been intrigued enough to try to find out whether someone named Thomas Dight ever actually lived at the Old Mint House. By most accounts, Dight only rented the property, making it almost impossible to find evidence of his tenancy.

'But someone wrote to me a few years ago,' Robert said, 'claiming that he might be a relative of his, as his name was Dight, too. It's a fairly unusual name. So there might be some sort of historical basis to the legend after all.'

One common manifestation at the Old Mint House is a white face that appears at the window above the door, with hands clutching frantically at the throat.

'Originally, I heard that people saw this only at night-time,' Robert continued. 'But someone sent me a letter in 2003, saying that they had gone to the pub, the Royal Oak and Castle, which is just opposite the house. It was the middle of the day, they were sitting outside with drinks, and they happened to look up to see this face at the window of the Old Mint House. They were so disturbed that they abandoned their drinks and went away.'

Unfortunately, the correspondent didn't include a name or address on the letter, so Robert was unable to find out more details. But most people who have seen a phantom at the Old Mint House agree that she is a woman who met a violent end there. Desmond Seward, writing in 1995, describes her as the 'tongueless female ghost who tries in vain to speak' and adds that Eleanor's shade had reportedly been seen in the house 'quite recently, certainly within the last ten years'.

Judy Middleton in *Ghosts of Sussex* writes that many people claim to have seen a female ghost in a haunted chamber on the ground floor. She relates an incident that occurred some years ago, when a man who was curious about the spooky tales spent a night in the room. To keep anyone from playing practical jokes, he locked the door and placed threads across the window. Thus settled in, he eventually fell asleep on a couch. Later, he was awakened by a strange 'metallic irregular' tapping coming from the window.

What he saw next gave him a shock - a woman's face was pressed against the outside of the diamond-shaped windowpane, staring in at him. He cried out, and the spectre passed effortlessly through the closed window to the foot of his couch. The man, although terrified, observed the ghost in detail. She was dressed in Elizabethan style, with a close-fitting bodice and a very full long skirt. Around her neck was a small ruff, and upon her head was a headdress of starched, stiffened lace.

After several excruciating seconds, the phantom glided back to the window. The man bolted for the door, to find his host and a friend. When the three returned to the Old Mint House, there was no sign of anyone there, and the threads across the window were still intact (Newbury, Berksire: Countryside Books, 1988, reprinted 1996, 39-40).

Andrew Green in *Haunted Sussex Today*, published in 1997, writes that the 'ghost of the young woman still makes her presence felt and quite recently heard' to members of the staff at the Old Mint House. One of them told Green that he 'really did feel that the young lady was with him in the room', and a twenty-year-old custodian reported having seen her while dusting artefacts there (Seaford, East Sussex: S.B. Publications, 1997, 62).

While there is apparently no connection between the haunting of the Old Mint House and that of its even more ancient neighbour, Pevensey Castle, it is clear that this beautiful and historic corner of Sussex has much to offer visitors on their search for the paranormal. They might do well, however, to keep a lookout for any Roman or Norman armies who might be marching by!

The Old Mint House outside Pevensey Castle's east gate

Preston Manor

BRIGHTON, EAST SUSSEX

In their hurry to get to the beach or to see the more famous Royal Pavilion, visitors to Brighton often overlook Preston Manor. This is a mistake that lovers of beautiful historic houses (not to mention intriguing ghost stories) should avoid. In a 1997 article for *The Lady*, I interviewed David Beevers, at that time Keeper of the Manor, who explained just why the property so deserves a visit.

'This house is unique,' he claimed. 'I know of no other typical Edwardian house open to the public in the whole of England. There are other houses of approximately this age, perhaps, but no other that exemplifies the typical taste of a gentry family at the turn of the century. Preston Manor is neither a stately home nor a modest villa - it somehow falls in between the two. At one time there were many similar houses, but they were eventually demolished because they became too big and uneconomic to run ('Preston Manor: an Edwardian time capsule,' *The Lady*, 16 to 29 December 1997, 78-79).

Preston Manor might have suffered the same fate or been turned into a casino or girls' school if its owners, Sir Charles and Lady Ellen Thomas-Stanford, had allowed it to fall into the hands of Lady Ellen's son, John Benett-Stanford. Instead they bequeathed the house to Brighton Borough Council upon their deaths in 1932 (Sir Charles' in March and Lady Ellen's in November). Since then, this rare survivor has been deemed a kind of Edwardian time capsule, still looking much as it must have done after the family made substantial additions and alterations to it in 1905.

Yet its history goes back much further. The name 'Preston', from the Anglo-Saxon 'Preste-ton', meaning 'a priest's farmstead', suggests that a settlement was here long before the Norman Conquest. When the Domesday Book was compiled in 1086, the property was one of eight manors belonging to the Bishopric of Chichester. It comprised most of the parish of Preston, many acres of what is now Hove, some two hundred acres of the parish of Bolney, and minor acreage elsewhere. In 1510 the bishop leased the Manor of Preston to Edward Elrington. The Elringtons and their relatives the Shirleys inhabited the property as leaseholders, first from the bishop and then from the Crown, until 1628, when descendant Thomas Shirley finally purchased it. Preston Manor was then handed down through more generations of the Shirley family until the early eighteenth century, when it passed through marriage into the Western family.

Structural alterations of the house were made in the latter half of the sixteenth century and again in 1738, when the Westerns incorporated some of the original foundations into the work. In 1794 Baron Western sold the manor and surrounding lands to William Stanford, who in 1841 passed the property to his son, another William. This William married Eleanor Morris a year later, and they had two children, a son who died in infancy, and a girl, Ellen, born in 1848. When William died, he left five-year-old Ellen to inherit Preston Manor.

Ellen's mother, Eleanor, married Captain George Macdonald in 1854. This union produced Ellen's three half-sisters: Flora in 1857 and twins Diana and Christiana (known as Lily) in 1866. When George Macdonald died in 1881, his widow, daughters and stepdaughter continued living at Preston Manor. Eleanor, in fact, lived there until her death in 1903.

In 1867 Ellen Stanford married her first husband, Vere Fane Benett. In accordance with her father's will, both Benett and Ellen's second husband, Charles Thomas, would obtain a Royal Licence to use the Stanford surname and to quarter the Stanford family arms with their own. Ellen and Vere lived with their son, John Benett-Stanford, at homes in Wiltshire, London, and Madeira, while Preston Manor continued to be inhabited by Ellen's mother and half-sisters.

Vere died in 1894, and three years later Ellen married Charles Thomas, member of a prosperous shipping family. In 1905 Ellen and Charles settled at Preston Manor, employing an architect who gave the property much of its present appearance. The house and its surrounding gardens today reflect mainly the personalities and idiosyncrasies of Lady Ellen and Sir Charles, but echoes remain from the long distant past.

Take, for example, the manor's most famous ghost. According to John Rackham's *Brighton Ghosts, Hove Hauntings,* the White Lady has appeared at intervals from the sixteenth century onwards, although she was most active during the late nineteenth century ('Preston Manor: Spirits of another age,' Brighton: Latimer Publications, 2001, 22-31).

At this time, she was said to appear about every six weeks or so, often enough that Lady Ellen's son John joked that the phantom had become a 'great friend' of his grandmother, Mrs Macdonald. Although John wrote to Henry Roberts, the first curator of Preston Manor, that he was 'not one of the people who are lucky enough to see ghosts,' he was nevertheless interested enough in the odd goings-on there to ask guests and family members to give accounts of their eerie experiences, hoping that the first guidebook to the property would contain them. The accounts apparently never made it into the guidebook, but fortunately they remain in the Preston Manor archives.

One of the family's earliest documented encounters with the White Lady occurred in October or November 1896, when Lady Ellen's half-sister, Lily Macdonald, was fitting a lampshade in the drawing room. Sensing that she was not alone, Lily turned to see a woman dressed all in white, her long, fair hair hanging down her back and her face looking pale and strained. The figure walked in through the door and towards Lily as if she were going to speak, but then moved past her without a word.

Lily had heard stories about the White Lady, and intrigued to see her at last, followed her through the billiard room as far as the foot of the stairs. When the phantom paused, Lily tried to put an arm around her, saying, 'No, you don't go now.' But her arm passed straight through the figure, which vanished in front of Lily's eyes.

Her twin Diana, who had also hoped to see the ghost, got her wish one evening during a tennis party. Having returned to the house at just past 6 PM to change into more comfortable shoes, she was halfway up the main staircase when she saw a woman standing ahead of her. Not recognising her as either a housemaid or one of the party guests, Diana greeted the stranger but received no reply. Intending to ask the woman to identify herself, she spoke again, extending her hand. Instead of meeting flesh and blood, however, her hand passed right through the figure, hitting the wall behind. In shock, Diana watched as the mysterious woman suddenly disappeared.

Friends of the Stanfords also encountered the White Lady. Lord Arundell of Wardour claimed to have seen her, as did Captain W.W. Sandeman and another military man, an army colonel, who was initially sceptical of the stories about the ghost. But one afternoon as the colonel walked across the entrance hall, the White Lady materialized in front of him. In astonishment, he asked her who she was and if he might help her, doubting whether an otherworldly being would have the power of speech. But speak she did, telling him that she was a nun who had been wrongly excommunicated.

But that was not her only problem, the White Lady insisted. When she died, she had been buried without proper ceremony in unconsecrated ground. She would find no peace, she warned, until her remains were reburied in a churchyard. Then, having given the colonel her message, she faded away.

As if to make it clear that the White Lady meant what she said, other unexplained phenomena were taking place at the manor during the same period. Two guests of the Stanfords had particularly unnerving experiences in the blue bedroom, today called the south-west room. In the first instance, family friend Mrs Studd awoke one night to the awful sight of 'a hand, without an arm' moving eerily up one of the posts of the four-poster bed. Terrified, she fled the scene to spend the rest of the night with Diana Macdonald Magniac in her room.

Likewise, a Mr R. Peregrine Burch had similar experiences in the south-west room, but he didn't write about them until September 1930, from his address at Apple Tree Cottage, Hare Hatch, Twyford in Berkshire. Describing the events of many years before, Mr Burch said he had heard 'most weird and uncanny noises' in the middle of the night, coming from inside the large dress cupboard. In one particularly unsettling instance, he heard loud taps on the cupboard door and the shuffling of footsteps. To keep anyone or anything from getting out, he 'barricaded' the cupboard door.

An even more horrifying experience so shattered the poor man's nerves that he was never able to sleep at Preston Manor again. One evening, suffering from a bad cold, he retired to the south-west room before dinner. Just before 10 PM, he was reading a book when the brass curtain rings on his four-poster bed began to jangle against one another. He also felt his bed being shaken. Laying down his book, he looked all around to see what could be causing the disturbance. To his horror, there appeared at the bedpost opposite him 'a man's dead arm and hand, with cruel fingers clutching the post and moving upwards'. He reacted just as Mrs Studd had done - he shrieked and leapt out of the door to the safety of another room.

Other alarming manifestations were also occurring. A new silk dress hanging in a cupboard in the south-west room was found to have diamond-shaped holes slashed into the fabric. The same thing happened later to two more dresses. Family friend Douglas Murray, writing a year or so after the events, referred also to the 'opening and closing of heavy mahogany doors by an invisible agency' and 'noises as of rolling tubs under the drawing room' when it was clear that no one was there.

Enough was enough. On 11 November 1896 the Stanfords held a séance with medium Ada Goodrich Freer in the Cleves Room, so named because a copy of a Holbein painting of Anne of Cleves was formerly displayed there. An ouija board or planchette was used to contact the spirit world, and details of the proceedings were taken down in shorthand and later transcribed.

The medium's first attempts to make contact were met with resistance, but she eventually received the response that two spirits, Agnes and Caroline, were haunting the house. The one speaking to the medium was Caroline, who identified herself as a nun with the surname of Marchmont. She was alive in 1535, she said, at a time when the manor was inhabited by someone named Marchant. Asked to clarify whether she meant 'Marchmont' or 'Marchant', the spirit answered confusingly that nuns had no name. When the medium asked what date the other spirit, Agnes, had died, the spirit snapped, 'Curse her!'.

Freer then asked Caroline why she hated Agnes so much. The spirit replied that Agnes, also a nun, had been excommunicated by the Church for serious misdeeds. Eventually Agnes herself spoke, explaining that in her day the manor had been used as a hostel for pilgrims on their way either to Canterbury or to a shrine called Winton-by-Sea. Agnes also mentioned a harbour called Whitebay, but neither of the latter two place names are recognised today anywhere in the area.

Then, in a startling development, Sister Agnes repeated the words that the apparition had spoken to the army colonel - that she had been wrongly excommunicated and then murdered as a result of jealousy between another nun and a monk. Even worse, she had been buried outside the manor in unconsecrated ground. The hauntings would cease, she insisted, only when she received a Christian burial.

A third spirit, Friar Martin, spoke next through the medium, admitting that he had been responsible for Agnes' excommunication. He confessed that he now knew that she had been innocent, the victim of lies that others had spread. But he assured the group present that peace would come to the spirit of Agnes sooner than she thought possible.

John Rackham, describing the séance in *Brighton Ghosts, Hove Hauntings*, comments on an interesting fact that the medium almost certainly would not have known, that by 1552 a man named William Marchant was the tenant of some sixty-two acres of the Common Laines, or farmland, that ran beside Preston Manor. Rackham ponders whether Marchant might have lived at the manor as the medium suggested (24-25).

Notes that were probably typed up by Henry Roberts, the first curator of the manor, indicate that in fact several séances were held, and that the sitters were told just where the nun's body lay - on the terrace outside what was then the dining room and afterwards the library of the house (now the Macquoid room). The Stanfords were sympathetic to the plight of the nun, but understandably hesitant to dig up the grounds 'on the off-chance of finding bones there'.

Just a couple months after the first séance, however, there was an epidemic of sore throats at Preston Manor. Fearing typhoid, the family called in a surveyor to inspect the drains, which had become dangerously blocked. On 29

January 1897 an incredible development occurred. As soon as workmen began excavating the drains, they found a skeleton in exactly the place that had been foretold during the séance. There was no trace of a coffin, but the bones had been enclosed in a very small space and placed in an unusual position, with the head twisted around and resting on the feet. To the observers, it appeared that the body had been disposed of hastily and without care.

When the Stanfords were notified about the unusual find, they invited a Dr Blaber to examine the bones. He identified them as having belonged to a woman of between forty-seven and fifty-five years of age, with 'perfect teeth'. The orange colour of the bones proved, he added, that they were at least three to four hundred years old.

The accounts of what happened next are somewhat confused, but apparently the vicar of the adjoining church, St Peter's, Preston, refused to allow what would have been a Roman Catholic skeleton to be buried in his churchyard. The Stanfords were determined to lay the woman to rest, however, and finally made arrangements with a gravedigger to bury the body in secret.

On 29 January 1898, one year after the skeleton was discovered, family friend Douglas Murray and Lily Macdonald held another séance in which a now pacified Sister Agnes came through to confirm that she was at last 'content to rest happily' but that she would continue to be a spiritual guide to Lily. On 10 December of that year, Douglas Murray wrote that in the nearly two years since the nun's body had been reburied, there had been 'no sort of phenomena at Preston Manor'.

That situation was not to last, however, for at about 8.30 on a July evening in 1903, Diana caught a glimpse of an unknown woman walking through the billiard room. Unlike the White Lady, however, this figure was dressed in black. As Diana watched, the woman made her way through the billiard room and into the drawing room, where she walked through the open French window into the garden. Diana ran to catch up with her, but found the garden empty. When she checked the gate, it was still locked, making it clear that no one of flesh and blood could have exited that way.

Just a few months later, in November 1903, the White Lady herself was to make another dramatic appearance, this time at the deathbed of her old friend. Mrs Macdonald had been ill for some time, and was being cared for in the south-west room, the scene of so much previous paranormal activity. Screens had been placed around her bed for privacy, and she was under the watchful eye of Nurse Glasspool. One morning between 2 and 3 AM, the nurse became aware that a woman in white with long fair hair was gazing intently around the screens at her and Mrs Macdonald. As soon as the nurse looked up, the woman had gone, but because of her fair hair, the nurse assumed that the visitor had been Lily, the only daughter of Mrs Macdonald to be staying in the house at the time.

Vexed that she hadn't spoken to her, Nurse Glasspool mentioned the incident to Lily at breakfast, asking in future that she say something when she entered the sickroom. 'It rather frightened me your coming in and not saying a word,' the nurse explained.

Lily knew that she had not come into the room the night before, but she didn't want to worry the woman looking after her mother. Nurse Glasspool had been kept in the dark about the spooky occurrences in the house. If she had known, the family reckoned, she might not have consented to work there. So Lily merely answered, 'Yes, certainly. I never thought you would be alarmed,' and agreed to speak to Nurse Glasspool the next time she came into the sickroom.

As Mrs Macdonald died shortly thereafter, on 28 November, some members of the family came to regard the episode as the White Lady's farewell visit to her friend. But it was by no means her farewell visit to the manor; in fact, she has apparently returned several times even in recent decades.

John Rackham describes a sighting that took place in 1976, when a Mrs Phelan visiting from Croydon was on her way to St Mary's Church in Surrenden Road. Passing Preston Manor, she noticed what appeared to be a nun dressed in white, standing on the lawn in front of the house. Mrs Phelan slowed down to take a closer look, but the nun vanished (*Brighton Ghosts, Hove Hauntings,* 28).

Rackham writes of another incident in 1992, when Anna Hinton, then aged thirteen, was being driven home from a dance by her father. The car turned into Preston Drove around 9.15 PM, and as it passed the manor, Anna glanced out of the window to see a woman in white. The figure was seated on a bench or chair and seemed to be either crying or praying, as she had her hands over her face. The evening was dark, with only certain parts of the house illuminated by streetlights. Nevertheless, the figure of the woman had a 'luminosity', as Rackham describes it, that made it stand out from the shadows. Anna Hinton continued staring at the woman as the car passed, but the apparition disappeared.

In July 2004 I interviewed Penny Balchin, who leads the extremely popular ghost tours at Preston Manor. She told me the story of one of the security staff, who about a week before his retirement in 2003 was showing around a visitor and his family. The visitor said that he had lived in the house as a child in the 1940s or 50s, when his father had been a caretaker there.

'He said he saw the White Lady loads of times,' Penny told me. 'One day he was riding his little bike up and down the corridor, and he climbed off it at one point. When he went back to ride it again, the White Lady was sitting on it.'

'The little boy told her, "Get off my bike!" and she disappeared,' Penny continued. 'He also said that she used to walk straight through a cabinet at the bottom of the stairs and disappear. This is the one where the fishing memorabilia from Norway are displayed now.'

Interestingly, Andrew Green in *Ghosts of Today*, published in 1980, writes that several visitors to the manor had told him of seeing 'a sort of white shape' close to the same area, on the staircase landing (London: Kaye & Ward, 47). Do these accounts suggest that the White Lady's spirit failed to find peace even after her body was laid to rest?

Penny Balchin reminded me of another, happier possibility. 'In the transcript of the séance held after the bones were reburied,' she recalled, 'the spirit of the White Lady came through to say that she would stay at Preston Manor as a guide. I have never mentioned this fact on the tours that I lead, but one day a medium in one of my groups told me that the White Lady was indeed still here in that capacity, serving as a spirit guide to help people.'

Another visitor who would probably agree with this interpretation is a Worthing woman whose letter to former Keeper, David Beevers, is dated 20 August 1984. Following a 'very pleasant and interesting visit' to the manor as a guest of the *West Sussex Gazette*, the woman went to bed at home later that evening and slept until 2 or 3 AM. Then she awoke and lay thinking of the manor, and 'instantly I was back there,' she writes, 'in a dark room'. Coming towards her was a 'dark grey figure or apparition of such rags and mortification.' The spectre came close to her and she 'looked on such a ghastly face,' with a nun's headdress all in tatters.

'I counted before I came,' were the phantom's strange words, and the writer suggests that this utterance probably refers to the nun's habit of counting her rosary beads. The ghostly mouth moved again, but no more words came. The writer noticed that the figure's hands were pressed close to its slightly crooked body. The nun then moved away, toward the garden, revealing more of her ragged habit.

'I was instantly at home again,' the letter writer recalls, 'wide awake and after such an experience a little bewildered.' But the vision had not frightened her, she insists. 'I have never believed in ghosts until then,' she continues, 'and feel she brought a blessing.'

It may be accepted knowledge now that the phantom known as the White Lady is none other than Sister Agnes, but the identity of the so-called Grey Lady of Preston Manor is much less certain. John Rackham writes that the first recorded sighting of this ghost occurred in the early twentieth century, when a housemaid looked through the window of the boiler-room, then in the basement of the house, to see a spectral woman dressed in grey (28-29).

This may be the same incident recalled by Penny Balchin, who told me that she heard a taped interview made in 1984 of a housemaid who was in service at the manor from 1920-23. According to Penny, this woman said that she used to see the Grey Lady regularly, not only through the boiler-room window but also in the downstairs corridor, where the ghost was known to walk up and down.

Penny believes that the Grey Lady might be the phantom of Sister Caroline, the nun who came through initially in the first séance of 11 November 1896.

Whoever she may be, the Grey Lady made her boldest appearances around the time of the Second World War. John Rackham writes that Doreen Rayner was one of several volunteers who saw her while on duty at the manor. Doreen was only sixteen when she joined the firewatchers, whose purpose was to keep an eye out for incendiary bombs hitting the house. Her job entailed going up onto the roof, and one night as she was on her way up, near the top of the staircase, she glimpsed a woman just ahead of her. The woman, according to Doreen, was wearing 'an old-fashioned grey dress' and 'seemed a bit misty in appearance'. As Doreen looked at her, the figure faded from view.

Shocked, Doreen nevertheless continued making her way to the roof, only to see the woman 'reappear by the parapet for a second or two before vanishing once more'. Doreen never saw her features, as the apparition was facing away from her. But as she explains in Rackham's account, 'I knew who it might be, of course, for I'd heard the others tell of a ghost.'

If we assume that the tales Doreen had heard were probably those of the famous White Lady, it's likely that that's whom she thought she was seeing. Yet Doreen's description of the phantom's apparel as 'an old-fashioned grey dress' sounds nothing like the nun's habit that we would expect the White Lady to wear. But then we must remember that many of the earlier accounts of the 'woman in white' make no mention that she was wearing nun's attire, either.

This same Grey Lady was observed again at the manor in the immediate post-war years. Rackham writes that two watchmen had been playing cards when one of them left to take a toilet break. While the other waited for his friend's return, he shuffled the cards in an aimless way.

Suddenly he became aware of someone standing behind him. Expecting to see his companion, he turned to face instead a woman in a long grey dress. Frightened, the night watchman rose from his chair to see the apparition disappear. His colleague, returning to the room, saw nothing out of the ordinary (28-29).

As well as a White Lady and a Grey Lady, Preston Manor also seems to be haunted by a Woman in Black. As we have already seen, a similarly clad ghost first made an appearance to Diana Macdonald Magniac in 1903. Whether this is the same one who appeared in 1993 to a security and information officer is not known.

In *Brighton Ghosts, Hove Hauntings*, John Rackham identifies the officer as Gerry Fleet. When I interviewed Preston Manor ghost tour leader Penny Balchin, she described Gerry as 'a big man, a union rep, not somebody who is a fly-by-night or who believes in ghosts'. Yet his encounter with the Woman in Black is something he will never forget.

According to Penny, Gerry came in to work around half past eight one morning and started immediately up the stairs to unlock the first floor rooms. 'He was halfway up the main staircase, when suddenly he felt like he'd walked into a fridge,' Penny told me. 'It was freezing cold, and the hairs on the back of his neck and arms stood up. As he looked up, he saw a lady in black come out of the south-west room. She crossed the landing and disappeared into the north-east room, through Lady Ellen Stanford's locked bedroom door.

'He said that she looked as real as you or I,' Penny recalled. 'There was a bustle at the back of her black dress, and her hair was in a bun. Gerry carried on with his unlocking, thinking that maybe someone unknown to him really was up there, or that he'd imagined things. But when he came downstairs, another staff member noticed how pale he was and that he had beads of sweat on his brow. She asked him, "What's the matter? You look like you've seen a ghost." And he said, "I think I have!"'

Penny added that Gerry, now retired, never saw anything unusual after that, but that another staff member has often noticed the shadowy figure of the Woman in Black, or rather her top half only, crossing from the desk to the window in the morning room.

No one has identified this phantom, but the bustle at the back of her dress indicates someone who was alive during the Victorian era. Might she not be the ghost either of Mrs Macdonald or one of her daughters, including Lady Ellen herself? One website suggests that the apparition of Lady Ellen has indeed been seen by a 'group of witnesses' as she walked through a wall on the outside of the house, but this figure was said to be dressed in white (http://www.paranormaldatabase.com/results.php). It is not clear why these witnesses were able to make such a positive identification. They may indeed have been correct, or they might possibly have seen the ghost of Sister Agnes and identified her wrongly as Lady Ellen (whose surname, incidentally, the website misspells as 'Stamford').

Ironically, Lady Ellen herself didn't believe in ghosts, and wrote to her son on 18 August 1930 that in her opinion, all stories about such things were the work of overactive imaginations. Yet no other resident of Preston Manor left so palpable an impression on the place - visitors today still claim to feel the presence of Lady Ellen all around them.

Other spirits inhabiting the house also seem aware of her continuing presence. In 1993, a security and information officer arrived for her morning shift. As soon as she began unlocking doors and opening windows on the ground floor, she distinctly heard a man's voice calling out, 'Ellie! Ellie, is that you?' The sound came from the direction of the drawing room doorway.

The security officer knew that she was the only person in the building; she had even re-locked the entrance door after arriving. Nevertheless, she made a thorough search of the drawing room and then the rest of the manor, but found no one. Reporting on this incident, John Rackham notes that if the voice was indeed of supernatural origin, it could have been calling for either Lady Ellen or for her mother, Eleanor Macdonald. Penny Balchin, however, told me that she was certain that the phantom voice was that of Sir Charles Stanford, calling for his wife, whom he was known to have addressed as 'Ellie'.

Supernatural smells, as well as supernatural voices, are reported at Preston Manor. 'We often detect the fragrance of lavender when none is about,' Penny said. 'I've smelled that myself, and in the morning room the scent is quite strong. We also frequently notice the fragrance of lavender wafting along the servants' corridors. There's no explanation for that, as we have had no potpourri or cleaning materials containing that scent.'

Many visitors on Penny's ghost tours also experience strange things. 'A medium came along once and said that she had seen a servant girl about sixteen years old in the dining room,' Penny recalled. 'The girl was wearing a blue dress, white apron and white mobcap. She also had clean hands, so she must not have been a scullery maid. This medium also detected presences in the Macquoid room.'

Not all phantoms perceived by visitors turn out to be the real thing, however. One visitor in 1975 was convinced he had seen the ghost of Lady Ellen's beloved 'Kylin', a Tibetan spaniel who died in the 1920s. The visitor was looking at pictures of the family pet when he saw what he assumed to be its supernatural counterpart scamper past him. This was no apparition, however, but a real, flesh-and-blood dog owned by the manor's custodian. He had so liked the looks of Lady Ellen's dog that he got one for himself.

While many eerie incidents at the manor have provoked bafflement or fear in those experiencing them, a few have stirred up even deeper feelings of disquiet. Staff member Kevin Bentman, for example, told me that many people report feeling 'uncomfortable, not very well' when entering two of the housemaids' rooms upstairs. Kevin's father, who works at the manor as a security guard, was locking up in this area one night when he felt an invisible someone touch his arm.

Kevin himself had a similar experience in the drawing room in March 2004. 'I was switching off the light under a cabinet,' he explained, 'and I felt a quick rush of cold wind blow past my right side. I turned around and there was nothing there. Then I felt a tap on my left shoulder. I was quite freaked out, so I rushed out of the room and told people, but they didn't believe me.'

That same day, Kevin added, visitors from a ghost tour were in the drawing room when one of the doors suddenly closed. Staff members weren't able to open it, so in order to leave the room, the group had to depart from another door. After the group had gone, the troublesome door opened easily. The experience 'added to the intense atmosphere of the tour,' Kevin said. 'A lot of the visitors thought we'd rigged it, but we hadn't.'

Ghost tour leader Penny Balchin gets the creeps when she goes down one particular staircase from the upstairs floor. 'I don't get these feelings anywhere else at the manor, but I don't like that staircase,' she told me. 'You often feel as if someone is behind you, so you keep looking over your shoulder. It's the staircase the servants would have used, and it's really steep. If I'm going up and then straight down again, I always leave the door open at the bottom. Lots of people have felt horrible things there, and you can hear footsteps.'

The north-west bedroom may also have an unsettling effect on those who enter it. Andrew Green, in both *Ghosts of Today* and *Haunted Sussex Today,* describes the 'mysterious sensation of unease' emanating from a corner of a triangular cupboard within the room. He and a group of students experienced the sensation for themselves during a 1978 visit, and Green claims that Marion Waller, former Keeper of the Manor, wrote to him after his televised appearance there to confirm that the north-west bedroom was 'often felt to have an unpleasant atmosphere'. A visitor to the room, Green writes, had attributed the bad atmosphere to 'the shameful activities of Lady Ellen Stanford who lived there until 1932' (*Haunted Sussex Today,* Seaford, East Sussex: S.B. Publications, 1997, 24-26).

Whether Lady Ellen participated in 'shameful activities' in the north-west room or anywhere else is a matter for conjecture, but as we have seen, it is the south-west room that has been the setting for the most alarming manifestations. Some of these, previously described, preceded the séance of 1896. But according to a confusing transcript typed up in 1935 by Lady Ellen's son John, one, if not two, of his mother's half-sisters also recorded terrifying experiences there.

According to the transcript, Diana Macdonald Magniac said that she was staying at Preston Manor in the spring 'of one of the early years' of the twentieth century. She had gone upstairs to sleep in what was formerly called the blue room at about half past ten. Just as the clock on the landing struck two o'clock, she woke up 'with a sense of fear'. A slight rustling noise seemed to come towards the bed, and the old nursery fender, transferred from another part of the house, began to shake and rattle.

Worst of all was her impression that something 'immensely evil' was leaning over her, sighing 'deep sighs which were almost groans'. Too terrified to move or even to open her eyes, she endured the ordeal for an agonizing few minutes before the noise and shaking ended and the presence seemed to move away. The rustling sounded again briefly near the door, the fender shook once more, and then there was silence. In a postscript, the writer adds that she does not know for certain whether the occurrence was reality or merely a vivid dream.

Most chroniclers of ghost stories at the manor have attributed this incident to Diana without further comment. But in John Benett-Stanford's typed notes, a confusing line appears immediately following the postscript, to the effect that 'she' - referring apparently to the woman whose experience has just been described - had had her first encounter with the supernatural when she was 'not [yet] ten years old, for it was before her twin sisters were born'.

This line cannot possibly refer to Diana, then, but must refer instead to her elder sister Flora, who was nine years old when twins Diana and Lily were born. When I contacted the former Keeper, David Beevers, to help clarify the matter, he replied that John Benett-Stanford was frequently confused with his facts and dates, and that the childhood incident the manuscript goes on to relate, following the fender-shaking ordeal, must, therefore, have happened to Flora Macdonald in about 1866, when she was nine years old. It remains unclear, however (at least to me), which sister was haunted by the rustling, rattling, sighing ghost in the blue room - was it Diana or was it Flora?

Whichever one it was, John Benett-Stanford's transcript goes on to describe an experience that so scared young Flora that, for many years afterwards, she refused to talk about it or even to enter the blue room again. Running down from the nursery (then on the first floor), she had seen the figures of two men struggling on the staircase, just a few steps up from the blue room. One of the combatants was dressed all in white except for a close-fitting red cap on his head. The other looked dark, although she couldn't see him plainly. Bewildered and afraid that the men would see her, she returned to the nursery, where the nursemaid thought she was ill and put her to bed.

On a few other occasions Flora was disturbed by unaccountable noises. One evening when her mother, Mrs Macdonald, had come in to say goodnight, the two of them heard what sounded like quantities of china or glass being hurled down inside a cupboard in the room. Mrs Macdonald immediately opened the cupboard door, finding nothing but dresses and coats inside. The same noise later awakened Flora. She also claimed to have seen the doors of various rooms burst open on windless days, and to have heard people say that it was impossible to keep the door of the blue room locked.

As Flora and her sisters Lily and Diana spent so much of their young lives at the manor, it would hardly be surprising to discover that they, too, have left psychic impressions there. Indeed, in November 2003, a security information officer identified as Susan wondered whether she might have seen the apparitions of two of them.

Susan normally comes in at midday to provide an opportunity for other officers to go for lunch. When she came on duty one day, three customers were waiting to be escorted down to the basement kitchen.

'As I walked them through the entrance hall,' Susan told me, 'I noticed two ladies on my left, by the pillars. I thought that they had just come into the house and that I would take them down for a tour later, after I had escorted the other visitors to the basement and back.

'These two ladies were of similar height, and they wore their hair swept back. They seemed to be in their 20s or early 30s, and both were wearing long dark clothes with long sleeves. One wore something on her top half that was pale grey. Their clothing didn't look modern, but it didn't cross my mind that there was anything strange about that, since we have people from two schools coming in each day, with the participants dressing up in Victorian or Edwardian clothes. These ladies were both looking at something that one of them was holding in her hands, perhaps a small book or leaflet. Although they were talking to each other, I don't remember hearing their voices.'

Susan continued showing her visitors around, then returned upstairs with them. There she met up with the two security guards on duty at the time. 'One of them asked me about the footsteps he'd heard walking across the floor upstairs, above the morning room,' Susan recalled. 'I told him that it must have been the two ladies who had been in the entrance hall when I went downstairs.

'They both looked at each other, and I said, "You must have seen them. You were both in the entrance hall when I saw them there." But they both insisted that they had not. I thought they were joking and made them search the house, because I was sure that the two ladies must still be inside. But the rooms were all empty.

'I still thought that the guards were teasing me, so I checked the till roll to find out how many visitors had been admitted into the house. That showed only the three customers that I'd taken downstairs.

'The guards swore that they weren't teasing me, so what did I see? I don't know,' Susan said. 'I just wish I had spoken to the ladies when I saw them. Lady Ellen died on the 11th of November 1932, so I wonder whether this might have been an anniversary of that date. She had three half-sisters, and I wonder whether the women I saw might have been two of them.'

Another unidentified phantom was apparently captured on film by photographer Tim Brown, who snapped a shot of the outside of the manor one clear night around 11 PM, when the house was illuminated by floodlights. The left side of the photo shows a figure that Tim describes as looking like a First World War guard, standing and holding a gun with the butt end resting on the ground. Around the head of the figure, Tim claims, are what appear to be 'fog demon faces'. To see the photo, visit http://theshadowlands.net/page12a.html.

The paranormal phenomena around Preston Manor are not limited to the house and grounds. The adjoining thirteenth-century parish church of St Peter can boast its own share of ghosts. Once the parish church of Preston village, the present building is believed to date from the time of Ralph Neville, Bishop of Chichester, who around 1226 was an occasional occupant of the manor.

Because the manor and the church have so much shared history, it comes as no surprise to learn that they probably also share a ghost or two. Andrew Green mentions that the 'ghostly form of a woman in white' has been seen by visitors and security officers not only on the manor grounds but also in the nearby church (*Haunted Sussex Today*, 26). And John Rackham writes that in 1968 a small booklet was produced for visitors about the history of the church, containing these words: 'Recently some members of the choir were emphatic that they witnessed a ghostly figure emerging from the south side of the church and disappearing in the churchyard' (*Brighton Ghosts, Hove Hauntings*, 30).

Was this phantom the famous White Lady of Preston Manor? Whoever she was, she wasn't the only one haunting the area. Rackham says that the historical booklet goes on to describe the experience of a couple of people walking past the church one Sunday evening. Two women in medieval costume appeared ahead of the walkers, then turned right, where they strolled through a tombstone on the west side of the church before disappearing.

Another couple in the 1970s were walking through the churchyard when they met a middle-aged woman clad in medieval costume. As she moved toward them and they had a chance to observe her dress, they assumed her to be a participant in a festival or pageant. They smiled and greeted her, but the woman didn't seem to notice them. The young man also thought it odd that she made no sound as she walked past. He and his companion both turned around to have another look, but were astonished to find that the woman had vanished.

Rackham writes of yet another unexplained occurrence from the 1970s, when Jacquie Reynolds and her friend were walking through the gardens near the church. They were taking an interest in the flowers when the apparition of a dark-haired woman suddenly appeared between them. This spectre, only about five feet tall, wore a long, plain white dress. She continued walking with the friends for a few steps before she, too, disappeared.

Inside the church of St Peter, a woman had two especially eerie encounters during separate visits, the first in 1992 and the second just over a year later. Rackham writes that the woman witnessed an unusual apparition gliding slowly along at the rear of the church. The figure seemed to be that of a woman wearing an old-fashioned, cream-coloured dress, but all that was visible was the back part of her gown as seen from the waist to the ample train at the bottom. The image moved along just a few feet before disappearing. On the second occasion, the same partially visible figure appeared in the part of the church immediately beneath the tower, where it disappeared through the tower base.

As female phantoms apparently abound near the church, I thought it odd to find no ghost stories about Celia Bashford Holloway. In 1831, Celia was murdered and dismembered by her bigamous husband in a house off Edward Street in Brighton. He then deposited some of her remains beneath the path called Lovers' Walk running near the churchyard wall. They were later re-interred in the churchyard, and a commemorative plaque was placed on the wall, wrongly stating that Celia had met her death nearby. None of the descriptions of the phantoms in the area match that of Celia, however, for the unfortunate woman had a most unusual appearance. Standing only four feet and three inches tall, Celia had a large head and long arms, with hands that turned outwards like the paws of a mole. Perhaps, having endured such a tragic life, Celia now enjoys real peace and has no desire to return to scenes of earthly misery.

My research turned up only two accounts of male phantoms haunting the church grounds. In the Preston Manor archives is a letter from an A.J. Greenaway, who claims to have seen the ghost of a friar outside the church in November 1929 or 1930. Might this be the shade of Friar Martin who during the first séance claimed responsibility for excommunicating Sister Agnes? Finally, Andrew Green in *Ghosts of Today* writes that there is a 'strong belief' that the phantom of Sir Charles Stanford, former Mayor of Brighton and husband of Lady Ellen, haunts the spot in the churchyard where his ashes are buried.

It seems fitting that Sir Charles might want to return to his former home from time to time, if only to see how much pleasure later generations are receiving from his and Lady Ellen's decision to bequeath it to the Brighton Borough Council. Visitors to the city today should repay that generosity by coming to see this unique historical treasure. As an added bonus, they might even be treated to a sighting of one or more of Preston Manor's ghosts!

The Priest House

WEST HOATHLY, WEST SUSSEX

f I were a ghost, I can think of no place I'd rather haunt than the charming, cosy Priest House near the Ashdown Forest in the village of West Hoathly. This early fifteenth-century timber-framed cottage was probably built for the monks of the Priory of St Pancras in Lewes, and modernised to become a yeoman's residence in the Elizabethan period, when it acquired central chimneys and a roof of Horsham stone. Surrounded by a medieval cottage garden with an abundance of old-fashioned flowers and medicinal herbs, The Priest House invites visitors to take a step back into the past.

But first they must step over the large iron slab serving as a threshold into the house. Believed to have come from a nearby sixteenth-century blast furnace, the iron threshold was meant to protect those within the cottage from witches, fairies, and other evil influences. According to a short article by C.F. Tebbutt published in 1980 in the journal *Folklore,* the belief in iron as psychic protection was widespread throughout England at the time. Tebbutt cites another example of an iron threshold at a seventeenth-century cottage in the adjacent Sussex parish of Danehill.

If witches, fairies, and demons weren't deterred by the iron threshold at The Priest House, they surely would be by the plenitude of ritual marks scratched into the timber beams throughout the building. Used to evoke Christ or the Virgin Mary, marks in the shape of letters, crosses, and daisy wheels were often gouged into timbers to protect occupants from spiritual harm.

'This is a house full of good luck charms,' curator Antony Smith told me. 'The beams are smothered with circular marks, lines, and scratched "V"s and "W"s. It's difficult to say when they were put there, but as there are a lot more of them on the museum side of the house than in the part I live in, it appears that they were placed there when the house was split into two parts, around 1700.'

Antony went on to explain that the village church also has anti-witch marks on its door, and another house in the village has a cat's paw wedged into the fireplace beam as a measure to keep witches away. 'You can see the claws sticking out - it's quite horrible,' he assured me. 'We also find boots and shoes buried in chimneys here, and you sometimes find mummified cats, mice, and rats - all sorts of things. I think I read that there were witch trials in East Grinstead at the end of the sixteenth century, so there must have been a local witch scare at that time.'

The iron threshold and ritual marks may have chased away all the truly evil spirits from The Priest House, but a former caretaker claimed that her pets used to sense something eerie about the staircase leading to the first floor. Florence E. Pettit, a visitor to the house during that caretaker's tenure, wrote in the early 1970s of her own 'sudden chill . . . shock of horror and repulsion' at the foot of the stairs ('A Woman's Psychic World,' unidentified source). She mentioned her strange feeling to the caretaker, who in turn admitted that she, too, disliked going upstairs after dark.

'There is something about that old staircase that my pets don't like,' the caretaker is quoted as saying. 'They follow me about everywhere, but they don't like that staircase and they won't come up after dusk, even if I'm still up there polishing. My dog just sits at the bottom and whines.' The caretaker went on to explain that she herself had never seen a ghost in The Priest House, but her animals seemed to do so often.

'When I'm sitting sewing and listening to the radio in the evenings, with the animals perhaps asleep beside me, they sometimes wake up and turn their heads in the same direction at the same time. It's very uncanny. It is just as though they are watching someone crossing the room. Sometimes the hair on my little dog's back bristles and he growls.'

Pettit's article goes on to suggest that the ghost haunting The Priest House might be that of Anne Tree, a martyr burnt at the stake in 1556 for her Protestant faith. Pettit had been told by a holiday relief vicar that several people had seen Anne's ghost crossing the village street on the anniversary of her execution.

There seems no reason to believe that Anne Tree's martyrdom has any direct connection to The Priest House, however, and present curator Antony Smith has lived there for sixteen years without any unusual occurrences.

'I know that one of the custodians back in the 1950s had troubles with someone knocking on the door outside,' he recalled. 'But when he went to check, there was never anyone there.'

Perhaps the iron threshold was just doing its job!

The Royal Pavilion

Royal Pavilion
BRIGHTON, EAST SUSSEX

Today's visitors to Brighton's Royal Pavilion might find it hard to believe that the most exotic, flamboyant showplace in the country was once described by poet Samuel Rogers, who dined there as a child, as a mere 'respectable farmhouse'. No illustrations are believed to have survived, but the modest original structure, marked on a late eighteenth-century town map, appears to have had two storeys and twin bow windows. This is what the house was like in 1786 when George, Prince of Wales, rented it from Thomas Kemp, Member of Parliament and father of the man who would go on to build Brighton's Kemp Town district. A year after moving in, the future George IV hired architect Henry Holland to incorporate the simple farmhouse into the grander neo-classical villa, called the 'Marine Pavilion', which featured a central domed rotunda and Ionic columns. In 1801-02 the building was enlarged by P.F. Robinson, and from 1815-23 it was transformed by John Nash into the ornate 'Indian Gothic' palace with Chinese interiors that we see today.

The biographer George Croly wrote that the happiest hours of George's life were spent in this home by the sea. Here he was able to relax in the company of his beloved Mrs Fitzherbert, the Roman Catholic whom he had married illegally and in secret, and who had her own house close by. George also delighted in hosting elaborate banquets and musical evenings at the Pavilion, attended by all the great and good of his day. Sadly, however, he was to enjoy his palace for only a few years after renovations were complete. Already in ill health by the time he ascended the throne in 1820, he began making fewer and fewer visits to Brighton, the last one in 1827.

After George's death in 1830, the Pavilion was passed on to his brother and heir, William IV, who used it more as a family residence than a venue for lavish entertainment. In 1837, William's niece Victoria inherited both the throne and the Pavilion, but is said to have disliked both the palace and Brighton itself. In 1850 she sold the Pavilion to the town commissioners for £50,000. By that time it was little more than a shell, having been stripped of most of its furnishings, and was used primarily for functions and exhibitions.

During the First World War, the Royal Pavilion and the adjoining Dome and Corn Exchange were turned into a hospital for more than four thousand Indian soldiers, some of whom, upon awakening for the first time to their glorious surroundings, believed that they had died and gone to paradise! Serious renovations to the Pavilion began in 1920 and continued throughout the twentieth century, interrupted by the Second World War, an arson attack on the Music Room in 1975, and damage from the storm of 1987. Over the years, the royal family returned many of the building's original furnishings and ornaments, enabling restorers to re-create the interior in all its former glory. Extensive structural work from 1980-92 likewise made the exterior as good as new.

Not surprisingly, one of the ghosts reported most often at the Royal Pavilion is that of George IV himself. Details are sketchy, but this phantom has apparently been seen several times in the underground passageway linking the Pavilion to the Dome, formerly the Royal Stables but now a complex consisting of a museum, theatre and concert hall.

Tall tales persist about a subterranean network of tunnels running in various directions from the Pavilion. One was rumoured to lead to the house of Mrs Fitzherbert on the Old Steine, while others were said to link the palace to locations as diverse as Western Road, the Clock Tower, and the Druid's Head pub. The more mundane truth, however, is that there is only one passageway, built in 1821 so that an increasingly unpopular George IV could make his way from the Pavilion to his stables and riding school (now the Corn Exchange) without being seen by the public.

Nevertheless, Andrew Green in *Haunted Sussex Today* writes that a number of people involved in the restoration of the Music Room in 1975 heard footsteps 'coming from the tunnel which leads to the Druids Head Inn' (Seaford, East Sussex: S.B. Publications, 1997, 21). Investigations were carried out, and although searchers found no explanation for the sounds, some of them saw the 'vague figure of a large woman in a dress, shawl and bonnet'. When they called out to her, she vanished.

Green wonders whether the phantom might have been that of Martha Gunn, the well-known bathing attendant whose job it was to plunge female clients into the sea as they emerged, modestly, from bathing machines. The rotund, robust 'queen of the dippers' held her job from about 1750-1814, a year before she died at the age of eighty-eight. A great favourite of George when he was Prince Regent, Martha had free access to the Pavilion kitchens. On one occasion she either stole or was given some butter, which she deposited surreptitiously inside her dress. The Prince Regent, having seen her sly move, teased her by edging her closer and closer to the fire as they talked, until finally the melting butter ran out of the poor woman's clothes and onto the floor!

While Andrew Green mentions the possibility that the ghost in the tunnel might instead have been that of Maria Fitzherbert, one observer of a phantom in the Pavilion's banqueting room had no doubts whatsoever about whom he had seen. John Rackham in *Brighton Ghosts, Hove Hauntings* recounts the experience of a caterer that took place at some time between the two World Wars. Shortly before the banquet was due to begin, he went into the dining area to make one last check that everything was in order. While he was there, he was suddenly surprised to see an 'elderly, rather rotund woman' coming from the direction of the kitchen. What startled him most, Rackham says, is that she was dressed in the style of another time. When the caterer was questioned later, he described the woman as wearing a long, 'bunched-up' skirt, triangular shawl and large bonnet. She seemed not to notice the presence of the caterer, but walked up and down the tables just as he had done, checking to make sure that all was as it should be.

The shocked caterer followed the woman, but when he was still twenty to thirty feet from her, she moved right through a closed door. He rushed toward it, threw it open, but found only an empty corridor. He then began running along the passage, and when he met an attendant, he asked whether he, too, had seen the woman. The attendant assured him that no one else had passed that way.

Convinced by now that he had seen an apparition and intrigued by who she might have been, the caterer looked through some old prints with Brighton themes. When he saw Martha Gunn's portrait on one of them, he insisted, 'That's her - bonnet and all!'

Rackham admits that the caterer may have been right in his identification of the ghost, although because of her seemingly professional concern around the tables, he considers it just as likely that she may have been a palace servant ('The Royal Pavilion and Dome,' Brighton: Latimer Publications, 2001, 32-33).

Current staff at the Pavilion tend not to want to talk about the supernatural, so for that reason I was impressed by the number of relatively recent accounts that Rackham was able to include in his book. Two of them involve Clifford Musgrave, director of the Pavilion for many years until his retirement in 1968.

Rackham explains that until the time of Mr Musgrave's retirement, private residential rooms took up an area on the top floor, part of which was later refurbished to contain the restaurant, while another part was converted back to the original Adelaide Suite.

Mr Musgrave and his wife were the last to live in these rooms before the renovations, and one evening, after finishing work and leaving his office, he walked through the Pavilion toward his residential quarters. He passed through a door and up a narrow flight of stairs. At the top, another door opened into a corridor. Mr Musgrave looked down it and noticed that his mother-in-law, visiting at the time, was just about to enter the bathroom at the far end of the corridor on the left. He continued walking along the passage and glanced left into the sitting room, thinking that his wife might be there. Instead, seated in an armchair and reading a newspaper was his mother-in-law! Wondering just who had gone into the bathroom, Mr Musgrave rushed back to find no one there (Rackham, 33-34).

The second eerie incident involving the Musgraves took place when a promotional film company was shooting scenes in the King's Apartments. At one point Mr Musgrave popped in to the set to say that he had to go out on business for a while, and he asked the producer to ensure that actors and crew stayed within the authorized filming area while he was gone. His business activities took less time than expected, and upon returning to the Pavilion, he heard screeches and laughter coming from one of the royal bedrooms, some distance from the area where the filming was going on.

Racing to the scene of the uproar, he was upset to find two actresses playfully wrestling upon a bed with crumpled bedclothes strewn about. Mr Musgrave ordered them out and after informing the producer about what had happened, he went to his flat and asked his wife to tidy the dishevelled bedroom.

Mrs Musgrave did just that, and as she finished, she ran her hand across the bedcover to smooth it out. Just then she had a strong feeling that someone was standing behind her, and she heard a low, male voice say, 'Thank you! Thank you!' Mrs Musgrave whirled around, but the room behind her was empty (Rackham, 34-35).

Rackham goes on to describe the experience of a female visitor in the mid-1970s who told her story to Flo Joinson, a Royal Pavilion attendant or 'warder', as they were called in those days. The woman said that her newly married brother and his wife had spent their honeymoon the year before in Brighton and had visited the Pavilion during the 'off-season' when there were few tourists. Interior photography was still permitted in those days, so the couple had taken several pictures of various rooms. One of the photos showed the banqueting room, temporarily emptied of its historical furniture.

The woman handed this photograph to Mrs Joinson, explaining that her brother thought he had been taking a picture of an empty room. Instead the photograph showed the top half of a man wearing what seemed to be a purple cloak with a white collar. Facing away from the camera, the man appeared either to have white hair or to be sporting a wig.

The woman gave Mrs Joinson her copy of the photo, assuring her that others had been taken from the negative. Mrs Joinson showed the print to several people, and while some believed it to be genuine, others considered it to have been faked. Mrs Joinson retired in 1980, and the photo unfortunately disappeared after being loaned to a young man who moved away without returning it.

Rackham also recounts two spooky encounters experienced by security officer Jacqui Chamberlain. At around 8.30 one autumn morning in 1991, Jacqui was walking up an iron spiral staircase in a storage area near the Adelaide Suite. As she looked through the apertures separating each of the stairs, she saw a male figure wearing drab brown clothing, perhaps the sort that a poor person from the Victorian era would have worn. Cringing in fear, the man acted as if he were hiding from someone. Before Jacqui had a chance to speak to him, he vanished. It was on the same staircase, Rackham adds, that the secretary of a former director of the Pavilion once saw the ghost of a woman wearing old-fashioned clothing.

Jacqui Chamberlain had her second eerie encounter one December night in 1993. This time she was walking through the King's Apartments when she noticed a man with dark, curly hair walking up a staircase in the vestibule area. His back was toward her, but she could see that he had on cream-coloured pantaloons and a shirt or blouse made from a silvery, satin-like fabric. Oddly, Rackham writes, the man seemed to be climbing an 'invisible' staircase. Jacqui learned later that one had in fact existed on the spot but was demolished in the early 1800s during the time of John Nash's transformations. After taking a few steps, the man vanished before Jacqui's eyes, leaving her to wonder whether she had just seen the ghost of the Prince Regent himself.

Rackham adds that several months later, a middle-aged woman, white-faced and trembling, approached a male security officer to report an extremely frightening supernatural encounter she had had in one of the ground-floor corridors. Unfortunately, she was too upset to give any details. With her was her husband, who claimed to have experienced nothing out of the ordinary, adding, however, that his wife was 'a bit psychic' (Rackham, 35-36).

About a year earlier, in the spring of 1993, another couple had reported a terrifying experience in the grounds outside the Royal Pavilion. Both young people, a Turkish man and a Swiss woman, were living in Brighton temporarily in order to learn English. According to Rackham, they had spent a few hours dancing in a West Street club when they decided to leave around 1.30 AM. They were on their way back to their student accommodation when they cut through the grounds of the Royal Pavilion. Just a few steps from the south gate they saw the black-cowled figure of a monk. The sight seemed to bring with it a 'strange, almost electric sensation,' Rackham writes, so that the couple knew immediately that they were witnessing something not of this world.

The next morning the young man described what they had seen to his teacher. The ghostly monk had stood quite close to them but remained motionless, his face and bare feet a 'slightly glowing white'. The couple had been so frightened that they couldn't move until the spectre disappeared. Rackham suggests that this might have been the same phantom seen occasionally in The Lanes and near the Brighthelm Church and Community Centre. He stresses that the foreign students' sighting of the apparition is especially significant, for with their poor English and limited contact with local people, they would most likely have had no prior knowledge of the ghostly monk (Rackham, 36, 54).

Likewise, a US group from Pennsylvania, the DelCo Ghosthunters, claim on their website to have had no knowledge of 'any real ghostly activity' at the Pavilion, although rather confusingly they admit to having heard that the phantoms of both George IV and Martha Gunn continue to be reported there. Nevertheless, group members were startled to find a large white misty spot in the centre of one of their photographs of the grounds in front of the Pavilion. To see the photo, go to http://www.delcoghosts.com/pavilion.html.

Supernatural activity in the vicinity is not restricted to the Royal Pavilion itself. A number of phantoms have been reported in and around the Dome complex, the royal riding stables constructed by William Porden in the early 1800s and modelled after the Paris Corn Market. The White Lady, which many observers say resembles Mrs Fitzherbert, is usually seen wearing a long white dress. John Rackham notes that some witnesses have described the ghost's clothing as grey, but concedes that there may be a second ghost. Indeed, Andrew Green in his *Haunted Sussex Today* makes no mention of a White Lady but refers briefly to a 'lady in grey' whose appearances are often accompanied by the sound of footsteps (Seaford, East Sussex: S.B. Publications, 1997, 21).

Rackham writes that the White Lady has been seen by many employees at the Dome, including an organist and several nightwatchmen, as well as by visiting entertainers who have seen her while they were rehearsing onstage. She has generally been seen in either the Stall Circle or balcony of the theatre. Security officer Peter Bourne, employed as a steward at the time of his sighting in 1984, gave Rackham the clearest description of all, that of a 'dignified, pale-faced woman with a bouffant hairstyle'. She was wearing a long, white, 'seemingly semi-transparent' dress, and she seemed to be walking slowly down a flight of stairs at the rear of the balcony. Peter explained to Rackham that this flight of stairs had long since ceased to exist, but he knew that they had once stood there (Rackham, 37).

On a warm summer day about six years later, Peter Bourne had an encounter with another of the Dome's ghosts. According to Rackham, an old information pamphlet describes this phantom as the Royal Coachman, although his appearance indicates that he might instead have been the Riding Master in charge of the royal stables. Peter was in an aisle near the centre of the auditorium when he caught a glimpse of what he first thought was an intruder entering the front stalls from the stage left door. Because of the Dome's central mercury lighting, he had an excellent view of a 'portly man' whose red, puffy cheeks and glaring eyes gave the impression that he was angry. Appearing to be almost seven feet tall, this flamboyant character was clad in a medium-brown jacket with a tail at the back, cream pantaloons with leather riding boots rising over the knees, a cream and white-coloured shirt with a frill at the front, a white waist sash, and a cream and brown diamond-patterned waistcoat with an attached gold watch-chain. Completing the outfit was a broad-fitting top hat with a dark feather in it.

Security officer Steve Mullings also saw the apparition as it reached the second of the balcony support pillars. Both men then watched as it walked to the fourth support pillar before fading from view (Rackham, 37-38).

Duncan Morrison, a steward, saw another phantom standing in the same area during the late 1980s. It was around 6.30 one night when Duncan, who was off duty, decided to watch the rehearsal of a visiting repertory company. As he was sitting in a seat near the front of the auditorium, he caught sight of another spectator wearing an old-fashioned lounge suit. Puzzled as to who the man might be but assuming that he was connected with the repertory company, Duncan turned to give him a closer look. After only a few seconds, the man in the lounge suit suddenly disappeared.

Rackham writes that Duncan was pleased to learn that a security officer standing at the back of the building had also seen the ghost in the lounge suit, but neither, apparently, had any idea who he was (Rackham, 38).

Another of the building's phantoms was witnessed by Mick Badrocke, who told Rackham that he had also seen the White Lady on several occasions. Mick, who retired after twenty years as a night porter at the Dome, once saw the ghost of a soldier in a red jacket with epaulettes and brass buttons. This spectre also wore tight-fitting black trousers and a tall black helmet that sloped slightly downwards from front to back. Mick also noticed a silver regimental badge above the peak of the helmet. This sighting occurred on the sundial stairs, so called because of their association with the roof architecture (Rackham, 36-37).

Rackham relates the tale of another night porter who, while walking around in the auditorium of the Dome suddenly found himself in an area that felt strangely cold. Spotting some coins on the floor, he bent to pick them up, but was then unable to straighten up again. This back problem was to remain with the unfortunate man for the rest of his life. Rackham admits that a draught might have been responsible for the cold area, and that the man may have had a latent back problem that just happened to emerge at that time. Nevertheless, the coincidence seems extraordinary (37).

Someone else who experienced a manifestation of a physical nature at the Dome was theatre technician Peter Hartley, who in the late 1980s was installing a ring intercom and show relay system. The job involved his squeezing into close spaces that were difficult to access, such as under the floor and inside wall cavities. At one point he and a colleague were working in an area near the orchestra pit, threading cable along a small hole that ran through a concrete support wall under the flooring. Rackham explains that Peter was standing on a ledge inside the cavity of a main wall, and his colleague was lying full-length on the other side of the support, so he could pull the cable through when it came out of the hole. Both men were working in the dark, with a trailing lamp to light their way.

Peter Hartley suddenly felt his skin prickling, and he became uncomfortably aware that he was not alone in his small space. Then he felt someone or something tug at his ankle, even though no one was there - in fact, there was no room for anyone else inside such a cramped area, and anyone making an approach along the cavity wall would have been detected instantly (38-39).

Besides these phenomena, footsteps made by an invisible presence have also been heard to walk across the Dome's stage, and the chain on the inside of the fire exit at the stage rear has been known to rattle mysteriously. Some might say that the ghosts in and around Brighton's Royal Pavilion are restless - so much so that they might even have spilled over into the Ha! Ha! Bar & Canteen just opposite the Pavilion entrance. That might account for the strange goings-on there in 2001, when - without assistance by live humans - glasses fell off shelves, lights switched off and on, and doors opened and closed. The ghost of a man even appeared on the stairs. Restaurant staff were so alarmed that they called in ghostbusters with web cams (see *The Argus*, 15 February 2001). But that, as they say, is another story!

Sackville College

EAST GRINSTEAD, WEST SUSSEX

In 1609 Robert Sackville, the Earl of Dorset, left money in his will 'to build a convenient house of brick and stone' to be used as an almshouse. This was the origin of Sackville College, which for many years also provided overnight accommodation for the Sackville family as they travelled back and forth from their estates in Sussex. This charitable foundation, now spanning five centuries, has been modernised for the comfort of its residents, but has always stayed true to its original purpose - that of affording elderly people a place to live.

And all of the original Jacobean charm remains. Visitors may tour the public areas of the College, including the Common Room, Great Hall with its gallery and original hammer-beam roof, Chapel, and Warden's Study. In this room the famous nineteenth-century Warden of Sackville College, the Reverend John Mason Neale, composed many well known hymns, including 'Good King Wenceslas'.

Hardly changed since Neale's death in 1866, the workplace even yet exudes all the cosy, contented atmosphere of a Victorian study - right down to the blue tobacco smoke swirling from the vicinity of the chair!

Tour guide Brian Evans told me that a past Matron of the College refused to enter the study, because, she claimed, 'We see blue smoke like that of tobacco coming from that chair - and it smells like tobacco, too.' The same woman said that the 'cleaning lady' had seen and smelled the smoke on several occasions and added that sometimes 'the temperature drops considerably, too'.

On the very day that I spoke to the present Warden of Sackville College, Graham Gaisburgh-Watkyn, the unexplained smell had returned. 'Just today my wife said to me that the tobacco smoke smell was there again,' he confessed. 'From time to time we smell it, coming from about head height from the chair in the study.'

If it is John Mason Neale returning in spirit form to enjoy the occasional smoke in his old chair again, this would apparently not be his only association with paranormal activity at Sackville College. Tony Wales in his *Sussex Ghosts & Legends* tells an anecdote in which Neale was crossing the quadrangle one day when the ghost of a recently deceased woman friend appeared to him. She begged Neale to talk to her husband to deter him from a crime he was about to commit. Neale did as the phantom asked and went to speak with the husband. Only by describing the apparition in detail was he able to persuade the man that it was truly his dead wife's desire that he refrain from committing the crime (Newbury, Berkshire: Countryside Books, 1992, 41. The story appeared earlier in F.G. Brabant's *Rambles in Sussex* published in 1909.).

Most of the strange occurrences at Sackville College seem to have taken place in the late twentieth century, however. Brian Evans related the tale of the wife of a past Warden, a lady 'whose intelligence and common sense' were beyond dispute. In the mid-1970s, when the College was the setting for a flower festival, some very large and heavy exhibition vases were moved during the night from their original positions in the hall and deposited onto the floor. They were discovered the next morning by the woman in question, who had personally locked up the hall the day before, and who was in possession of the only key.

Could the vases have been moved at the behest of the beautiful young 'Lady in Blue' who occasionally put in an appearance towards the end of the twentieth century? This ghost, according to Brian Evans, was glimpsed through the windows of the dining room used by the Sackville family in the seventeenth and eighteenth centuries.

Another story from the mid-1970s involved two elderly residents of the College, both now deceased. They lived in separate quarters on either side of a large room just above the Common Room, decorated with an ornate ceiling and chandeliers. This area had probably been used by members of the Sackville family to entertain guests. Both women, on different occasions, said that a hand, or hands, had come through the wall from the large room and attempted to push them out of their beds.

A decade or so later, in 1987, a resident described by Brian Evans as 'well balanced and free of susceptibility' said that she 'was often visited by an old lady in a long white garment who would sit on the end of her bed'. From this woman's description, the visitor was identified as a previous resident who had occupied the same room until her death twenty years earlier. The 1987 resident was asked if she was afraid of the apparition, to which she replied, 'No, why should I be? She never hurts me, never speaks, just sits and then quietly vanishes after a while.'

So it would appear that the Earl of Dorset's 'convenient house of brick and stone', Sackville College, may be just as much an almshouse for denizens of the spirit world as for its flesh-and-blood residents!

Sheffield Park Garden
UCKFIELD, EAST SUSSEX

ew ghost stories in Sussex are simultaneously so well known yet so vague as that of the headless woman spectre of Sheffield Park Garden. This National Trust property, a paradise for nature lovers at any time of year, has christened some of its principle features in her honour. The Upper and Lower Woman's Way Ponds both take their names from the original 'Woman's Way', a stepping-stone path over which the ghost was said to walk. The Cascade Bridge was later built over the site of the old stones, but that didn't seem to put the lady off, as she has also been seen crossing the bridge, vanishing if anyone approaches her.

The phantom is so famous that she even gets a mention in the guidebook, so it seems odd that no one knows who she is, much less why she's missing her head. One version of the legend is that she's doomed forever to walk around the ponds, but it doesn't say what she did to deserve such a fate in the first place.

When I spoke to a man in the gift shop in 1997, he said that staff members jokingly referred to the ghost as 'Esmeralda' and blamed her whenever something out of the ordinary occurred. 'We have items falling from the shelves sometimes - that kind of thing. Nothing that couldn't really be explained away,' he insisted.

The current visiting services and marketing manager, Joann Hopkins, told me that one night a gardener thought he saw an apparition, but later put the sighting down to foggy conditions and bad lighting. Joann also mentioned that a woman once claimed to feel a presence in the mansion.

'Our understanding of how the ghost manifests itself is very sketchy,' said manager Sue Medway. 'To my knowledge, there haven't been any recent experiences of people coming into contact with her. Although, obviously, the fact that the story has lasted this long must mean that it's based on something.'

One theory is that the tale of the headless phantom was created, or at least was conveniently used, to frighten young housemaids from skipping out in the evenings to fraternize with local village lads. 'It was certainly a way of keeping some of the young ones at home,' Sue explained. 'The house is only about a mile from the village, and the way is across the bridge that the ghost is said to haunt.'

Unfortunately, the house is not open to the public, but visitors may wander freely in the landscaped gardens laid out by 'Capability' Brown in the eighteenth century and further developed by owner Arthur Soames in the twentieth. There's always the risk of running into the headless lady, of course, but if you do, at least try to find out who she is before she disappears!

Southover Grange Gardens
LEWES, EAST SUSSEX

uilt probably in the late sixteenth century, at least partially from Caen Stone taken from the remains of nearby Lewes Priory, Southover Grange was where the famous diarist John Evelyn spent most of his childhood. In the nineteenth century, Harrison Ainsworth used the setting for his novel *Ovingdean Grange,* renaming the building Mock Beggars' Hall.

While the Elizabethan house is not open to the public except for weddings and other important functions, the surrounding garden, with its stately trees alongside traditional and contemporary flower displays, is a welcoming oasis for visitors year round.

The gardens have been the setting for at least one paranormal incident, described by R. Moore in *Sussex Ghosts* (St. Ives, Cornwall: James Pike Ltd, 1976). At some time in the mid-1970s, shortly before Moore's book was published, a woman who took a photograph of the gardens during a spring flood was astonished by the results. Clearly discernible in the developed picture was what appeared to be the shape of a man rising out of the water, carrying something on his back.

More traditional spooky incidents have occurred inside the house. Caretaker Jan Larkin told me that when she is trying to work in the early morning, she hears footsteps walking to and fro 'all the time'. 'I usually say, "Come on! Instead of spying on me, come down and give me a hand!" Oddly enough, this happens only when the flat upstairs is empty - whenever people actually move in up there, I don't hear a thing. It's very strange. There's definitely something there, though, because a friend of mine who is a white witch said he felt a presence. And when my dog goes into the building, he can't wait to get out. He'll stay for only a few minutes before going to stand at the front door wanting out. He doesn't like it in there at all.'

Jan doesn't know who the ghost may be, but she described another incident when an apparition was actually sighted. A group of nursery school children were sitting in the front entrance hall, and a little girl kept looking up at the window on the stairs and waving her arm. The teacher finally asked her what she was doing, and the little girl replied, 'There's an old lady up there who keeps waving to me.'

Certainly there is nothing sinister about any of the unexplained incidents at Southover Grange, and after all these centuries, its gardens remain the perfect spot to picnic or simply to stretch out under the trees for a short rest.

St Mary's

BRAMBER, WEST SUSSEX

It's frightening to realise just how close the charming St Mary's in Bramber came to being demolished near the end of the Second World War – not by enemy bombs but by one of its own countrymen! But if an extraordinary coincidence hadn't brought this fifteenth-century monastic inn to the attention of the right buyer at the right time, that's exactly what would have happened.

One day in 1944, while Dorothy Ellis was visiting her hairdresser's in London, she happened to see a magazine advertisement about the upcoming sale of St Mary's. After reading the history of the house, she knew she had to have it. Well-meaning friends tried to talk her out of it, but Dorothy went anyway to the auction at the Old Ship Hotel in Brighton. Once there, she was horrified to learn that the local builder bidding against her wanted to tear down St Mary's in order to re-use the timbers!

Fortunately, Dorothy was able to outbid him, and just in the nick of time, she became the saviour of one of the most remarkable historic houses in Sussex. For the once-beautiful St Mary's, built in 1470 by the Bishop of Winchester on an even earlier Knights Templar site, had become dangerously dilapidated. The panels in the Painted Room were scratched and scarred, ivy was growing inside the Music Room, and wall coverings throughout the house were torn, filthy, and collapsing onto the floor. Perhaps the worst damage had occurred when St Mary's was requisitioned by the Ministry of Defence as a billet for Canadian and Scottish troops during the Second World War. Staircase treads and electric cables showed wear from heavy military boots, remnants of the soldiers' food were scattered everywhere, and in the hall, someone had used red paint to scrawl 'Home Sweet Home' in twelve-inch-high letters on the wall.

For the next thirty-five years, until 1979 when advancing age finally forced her to sell it, Dorothy Ellis restored, protected, and preserved St Mary's for the future, as well as opening it to the public. Visitors to the property today - not to mention its ghosts - owe much to that chance occurrence of a woman visiting her hairdresser's, just as they do to current owners, Peter Thorogood and Roger Linton, who bought St Mary's in 1984.

At that time, the house was about to be purchased by a commercial organisation and closed to the public, so members of the Thorogood and Linton families, because of their friendship with earlier occupants the McConnels, joined forces to save St Mary's once again. They continued the restoration work and report that the house now has a positive, warm, and welcoming atmosphere.

'Probably the monks who were here had a good influence on it,' Peter Thorogood told me, referring to the time when St Mary's was thought to have been occupied by four monks belonging to the Priory of Sele. 'They were rather a jolly crowd, I understand, from what records we have. I think the house was even closed down for riotous behaviour on one occasion!'

The monks enjoyed themselves so much, in fact, that they just might have decided to stay on. Or perhaps they recognised kindred spirits when the house was full of boisterous, young military men during the war, so they returned to participate in the revelry. Whatever the case, the Canadian soldiers billeted at St Mary's reported a spectral monk strolling along the appropriately named Monk's Walk, and some visiting land-girls also claimed to have witnessed certain 'manifestations', although unfortunately they left no details. An underground tunnel leading to the church of St Botolph's in Upper Beeding is said to pass beneath the South Garden, and unexplained loud knocking on a doorway admitting to this passage was sometimes heard. Attributed to the ghosts of those long vanished monks, the mysterious thuds have not been heard for a long time now, however.

Along with tales of the phantom monks, the new owners have inherited plenty of other ghost stories, too. As Peter Thorogood explains, 'The north attic is always very cold, and we heard that someone who used to sleep there, perhaps a servant, would occasionally have the bedclothes ripped off him while he was in bed. And visitors tell us on occasion that the King's Room, where Charles II is supposed to have hidden during his escape through Bramber, is very cold, and that they've felt a presence there. A secret door has been cut in the wall for a secondary escape route, and there's a priest hole behind the chimney, so I suppose that the room does have certain vibrations.'

Peter recalled a time before he came to live at St Mary's, when a psychic lady told residents of the house that if they looked hard enough, they would find something hidden in the room. 'When we came,' Peter said, 'there were holes all over the walls where they had been searching for whatever this hidden thing was, and in doing it, they pretty well ruined the fabric of the room. The ceiling had nearly fallen down, and there were holes everywhere that we had to fill up. Of course, there may still be something hidden there - we don't know, but we certainly haven't looked for it.'

Peter's sister Mary Thorogood wasn't looking for anything, either, but one day in the 1990s she found something shocking when she went to do some hoovering in the area of the private apartments. She was outside the door to the Painted Room, which has connections to Queen Elizabeth I, when she noticed a small child looking down at her from the top of the stairs.

'The child was smiling in a rather cheeky way, dressed in Elizabethan costume, with a tunic, a ruff, and a black velvet hat with a feather,' Peter told me. 'Later we found the Hoover where my sister had left it, and when we asked her about it, at first she said she had just decided to stop working. But later she told us what she had seen, and was quite adamant about it. She had no idea who the child might have been. She said that she wasn't frightened, but that she just hadn't wanted to disturb anything.'

Another phantom, a lady in grey, was reportedly glimpsed from time to time on the main staircase by Mimi McConnel, who lived at St Mary's from 1915-1938. 'Mrs McConnel was a great friend of Irene Bonnett Swann, my Aunt Bunny,' Peter explained. 'They were up at Cambridge together, and that's how our family got a link with the house. Mrs McConnel was quite psychic and saw the grey lady several times on the stairs, but no one has seen that ghost since. Another story we heard is that Mrs McConnel used to send lighted straws or paper up the big inglenook chimney in the monk's parlour downstairs, hoping to bring spirits down.'

Probably the most common unexplained occurrence at St Mary's is the mysterious fragrance of roses, detected in various parts of the house. 'Roger Linton's father, the Reverend Laurence Linton, was woken up by the smell in the night, in the room above the Painted Room,' Peter Thorogood remembered. 'He said it was a very powerful, sweet, herby rose smell, rather like potpourri, but none was in the house to account for it. That bedroom is mine, and I have never smelled anything there. But Roger's mother, Renee, smelled it on the landing outside the Painted Room, and that was quite powerful, too. She was also woken up by the same smell on another night, in the room above the Painted Room.'

Besides its supernatural connections, St Mary's has an interesting assortment of literary ones as well. Research by the present owners has revealed that the house was probably the setting for Sir Arthur Conan Doyle's short story, 'The Musgrave Ritual', in which Sherlock Holmes is summoned to an ancient house in West Sussex to find the butler dead in the cellar, still clutching the treasure left behind for safekeeping by Charles II on his escape over Bramber Bridge (an Alfred Musgrave was the owner of St Mary's around the time of Conan Doyle's writing). And Algernon and Gwendolen Bourke, who lived at St Mary's in the 1890s, were the inspirations for two of the principal characters in Oscar Wilde's *The Importance of Being Earnest*. The literary connection continues at St Mary's today, as present owner Peter Thorogood has the largest collection in existence of the works of nineteenth-century poet and caricaturist Thomas Hood. The charming house and grounds have also been the setting for various television programmes, including *Doctor Who*.

But of all the marvellous stories, both fact and fiction, associated with the property, none is more miraculous than the one about how fate stepped in to a London hairdresser's just in time to save St Mary's from destruction.

Uppark

SOUTH HARTING, PETERSFIELD, WEST SUSSEX

ollowing a devastating fire on 30 August 1989, Uppark was lovingly repaired and restored by a massive team of architects, contractors, and craftsmen under the aegis of the National Trust. Sadly, the upper floors containing the Meade-Fetherstonhaugh family possessions could not be saved, but the rest of the seventeenth-century country house was returned as fully as possible to its former glory and reopened to the public on 1 June 1995.

A current member of staff claimed not to know anything about spooks at Uppark, so one can only hope that the mansion's charming ghost survived both the flames and the restoration. But three years before the fire, in 1986, Peter Underwood chronicled some strange goings-on at the property in *This Haunted Isle: The Ghosts and Legends of Britain's Historic Buildings* (Javelin Books: Poole, New York, Sidney, 187-89).

Underwood identified the spirit-in-residence as former owner Sir Harry Fetherstonhaugh, whose father purchased the estate in 1747. Sir Harry is probably best remembered today for the women in his life. In 1780 he began an affair with Emma Hart, the future Lady Hamilton and lover of Lord Nelson; and in 1825, when he was over seventy, he scandalised conventional society by marrying his twenty-year-old head dairymaid, Mary Ann Bullock.

Sir Harry died in 1846, leaving the house to his widow, who lived until 1874. Mary Ann's companion was her sister Frances, who assumed the Fetherstonhaugh name and continued on at Uppark until her death in 1895. She bequeathed the estate to Colonel Keith Turnour-Fetherstonhaugh, who in turn left Uppark to the Meade-Fetherstonhaughs. Some members of this family continue to live there today, in spite of turning over the property to the National Trust in 1954.

Any of those who graced Uppark in the past could have returned there in spirit form, but Underwood is certain that the ghost wreaking playful havoc in the Red Drawing Room was none other than Sir Harry. Mysterious sounds were reported, along with windows that opened and closed, seemingly on their own. But weirdest of all was the behaviour of an antique firescreen, placed in front of a fireplace and directly under Batoni's portrait of Sir Harry as a young man.

When Underwood visited Uppark in 1981, the administrator, John Eyre, told him that whenever the firescreen was placed the wrong way round, it would later be found to have reversed itself to the proper position. When the firescreen was taken away for repairs, Mr Eyre put in its place an antique desk that incorporated a sliding firescreen. Each day he made sure to raise and carefully fix the screen at an appropriate height, only to find it lowered again the next morning!

Intrigued, Mr Eyre arranged for the screen to be wedged open at a certain height, but it was still found in a lowered position the next day. Eventually a carpenter fixed the wedges, making it impossible for the screen to be moved at all. Such a tactic seemed to inhibit the ghost, at least temporarily, but Mr Eyre was hoping to perform further experiments as soon as the original firescreen returned.

It would be interesting to know the results of those experiments, and even more interesting to know whether Sir Harry's ghost still takes up residence at his beloved Uppark!

Verdley Castle
NEAR FERNHURST, WEST SUSSEX

Verdley Castle might be considered something of a ghost itself, now that traces of its existence have all but disappeared. The thirteenth or fourteenth-century fortified hunting tower was in ruins as early as the 1500s, and most of what remained was quarried by local builders before the site was finally demolished sometime in the eighteenth century. Yet this remote spot in Verdley Wood, at the bottom of the north slope of Henley Hill, is said to be the haunt of the ghost of the last wild brown bear to be killed in Sussex, if not the whole of England. Felled by a hunter's bow during the Middle Ages, the enraged bear is said to roam the woods in spirit form, protesting its cruel slaughter.

According to the legend, reprinted in an article in *The Herald* on 13 August 2004, the bear was looking for food one snowy Christmas Day when a group of yokels came upon it. The frightened animal sought refuge inside Verdley Castle, but was hunted down and slain inside the great hall. It is said that the growls of the bear, as well as the shouts of the hunters, can sometimes still be heard at Christmastime.

The story is little known even by locals, but it has been mentioned in at least a couple of books. The tale piqued the interest of an Australian film company, Storyteller Media Group, who visited Verdley Woods in August 2004. The crew spent one Thursday evening filming six psychic mediums and two historians near the site of the old Verdley Castle, hoping to catch a trace of the phantom bear for their *Animal X,* a programme on animal ghosts.

According to Judith Turner's article in the 19 August 2004 *Midhurst and Petworth Observer,* the mediums had done no research on the area and were not told why the film crew was there, in order to prevent their being subconsciously influenced. Local historian Nigel Headland and West Sussex county archaeologist Mark Taylor watched the mediums on closed circuit television and commented on their progress. Over the course of the evening, the mediums reported on a variety of sensations involving the ruins, but no one sensed the presence of a bear. But as the legend says, this animal ghost returns only at Christmastime, so perhaps it's no wonder!

Wakehurst Place
ARDINGLY, NEAR HAYWARDS HEATH, WEST SUSSEX

With its year-round famous gardens sporting native and exotic flowers and trees, woodland and wetland walks, and the remains of its 1590s manor house, parts of which are open to the public, Wakehurst Place seems to have everything going for it. Everything, that is, except a really interesting ghost story!

At least that's what the ranger Veronica Withall told me. Apologising for the scarcity of supernatural occurrences at this National Trust property managed by the Royal Botanic Gardens in Kew, Veronica went on to say that a grey lady of unknown identity has been seen on more than one occasion by people working upstairs in the old part of the mansion. And then there's the unaccounted-for smell of cigar smoke sometimes detectable downstairs in the hall, mainly in the autumn.

Veronica seemed genuinely sorry that Wakehurst Place didn't have more to offer in the paranormal department. Perhaps spooks searching for a new haunt would care to apply?

About the Author

Debra Munn, a long-time Anglophile and native of Amarillo, Texas, moved in 1995 to Brighton, where she lives with her husband, Mick Henry. Debra has a Ph.D. in American literature from Florida State University and has published short stories, essays and articles on a variety of subjects. She is also the author of *Ghosts on the Range: Eerie True Tales of Wyoming* and *Big Sky Ghosts: Eerie True Tales of Montana* (Volumes One and Two) published by Pruett Publishing of Boulder, Colorado. In addition, Debra is the creator and marketer of couple*connect* relationship enhancement cards.